WHAT IF YOU DON'T WAKE UP ALIVE TOMORROW MORNING?

The Beginning of the End!

notionpress
.com

WHAT IF YOU DON'T WAKE UP ALIVE TOMORROW MORNING?

THE BEGINNING OF THE END!

GAVIN D'SOUZA

notionpress.com

Notion Press

Old No. 38, New No. 6

McNichols Road, Chetpet

Chennai - 600 031

First Published by Notion Press 2016

ISBN 978-93-5206-777-0

Was it all an accident or am I really the chosen one?

- Gavin D'Souza

The pages are still blank, but there is a miraculous feeling of the words being there, written in invisible ink and clamouring to become visible.

-Vladimir Nabokov

Thank you for your valuable time, constant support and never-ending patience. Thanks for lighting my path, trusting me and tolerating me. Thanks most of all for your unbelievable understanding, hardcore honesty and your sweet ever-lasting LOVE. This book would have been just a dream without YOU…

- Señorita, my Billu!

Inspired by the

Events on September 29, 2011…

In the loving memory of
My grandparents and
Pramod Kumar Vajran

Dedicated to

Ravi Kiran (on the right)

(03.07.1990 – 29.09.2011)

A Very Special Personal Thanks To

All of the gods out there, the Big Bang, the universe, space, the Milky Way galaxy, the solar system, the sun, the moon, the earth, nature, life, gravity, oxygen, food, water, chai-cigarette, my black gel pen, my empty book, the twenty-six English alphabet, English language (my favourite language is Kannada though!), my brain, my thoughts, my parents, my school, the education system, my teachers, my classmates, my childhood friends, the hostel wardens, my neighbors, my former enemies, ex-girlfriends, crushes, all the machas and magas, bros, dudes, babes, college mates, smoking friends, Dew Heights apartment friends, office friends, friends from here, friends from there, electricity, technology, internet, Google Chrome, Google, Wikipedia, Word hippo, Facebook, WhatsApp, Blogger and my laptop!

Thank you Bill Gates for Windows and Microsoft Word, but not for Internet Explorer. Thank you music, Linkin Park in particular, movies, all the beta readers, editors and publishers. And last, but not the least, you - the reader. The list of people and things I would like to thank is too long that I would need an entire book. So let me stop here and move on.

The People!

Well, whom do I start with? Where do I begin? Okay, let me follow some arbitrary pattern. This is not in accordance to my preference or their performance. Kevin (aka Cavi), Ashma (Ampa), Ashmitha (Mittu), Girish (Sisya), Arjun (Macha), Gayatri (Gayaaa3), Parul Pant (Paruuu, Angry Bird), Sudheer (Dynamite), Prabhakar (Macha), Partha (Mr. Bean), Sandy (20 minutes, Macha), Kiran (Kido) Jibin (Praise the Lord), John Bosco (No Problem), Sagar (The Mentor), Hari (Intel, AMD Inside), Praveen (Punith/ Boss), Gafur (Bhai), Jacil, Danisha (Kanyakumari), Bharath (Maama), Mahesh (Muzik), Desmond (King Solomon!), Karthik (Apple) and Reezal (Petrol). And all the others I have missed naming.

Writing this book wasn't a random miracle.
I just decided to write and I wrote.

-Gavin D'Souza

All the characters in this book are non-fictional. Any similarity or resemblance to any person, living or dead is purely…

INTENTIONAL.

The Few First Words...

Many people are responsible for the successful completion of this book. My parents for their blessings and belief in me. My brother for his tips, suggestions, corrections, arguments and for proof-reading this book. I have had the support of my cousins, encouragement from relatives, feedback from friends, love from ex-girlfriends, stares of strangers and the efforts of editors, publishers, the smart and kickass marketers, sellers and distributors. Competition from rivals and praises from enemies have also made this final product a reality. I am just the writer! *(Trying to be humble!)*

I would also like to thank the God Almighty, the king of kings, for magically making all these words appear on paper. Last, but not the least, a big thank you to all the naysayers who said that I was mad and stupid, that I wouldn't make it and that I would fail. Thanks a million! I did it! I cannot believe that I have completed this book. It is unbelievably amazing. I am officially a writer now. This feels so magical and miraculous. You know what I am sayin'?

The Dis-claimer

The words penned down in this book are mostly mine. They are products of the thoughts from my brain. Some words may have been uttered by others, alive or dead. They may be from the nuggets I have read or heard in group conversations. Some half-truths may be from text messages, headlines in the newspaper or the internet or 'breaking news' on television.

All facts, figures, statistics, definitions, data, analysis, reports, research and history are from Google, Wikipedia, YouTube and thousands of other websites. I have also derived inspiration from good books written by great authors, articles, blogs, movies, documentaries, text books, magazines, serials, advertisements, music, FM radio, my parents, relatives, friends, strangers and just about everyone and everything. I have questioned, argued, understood, analysed, verified, simplified and utilised everything that I have heard and read. I have tried my best to credit all my sources. I have made an earnest and honest attempt to nail the truth better than I can. I haven't stolen anything from anyone.

I honestly do not know where all these words came from.

I am sorry if I have gone wrong somewhere.

Welcome to My World

Obviously, I miscalculated a few things. When I started writing this book, there were several questions buzzing in my head. Who could I ask? Who is the right teacher? Where do I find the answers and the evidence? How should I discover the truth? Do God and heaven exist unceasingly or is it just the Big Bang that created everything? When and where did it all start? What is the end? How enormous is the universe? Is He watching us from the stars?

People often tell me, "Wow, you have the talent to write a book!" You don't need talent to write a book. You have to believe that you can write. All great authors believe they can and they write. The ideal engineers create. Doctors save lives. Writers write. You are reading the 22nd version of this book today. It has been revised over and over to get to the stage where it is today. Am I trying to prove anything? NO! Not a thing. This isn't a testimony to anything that exists out there. You cannot use this book as evidence for anything – good or bad. You don't have to agree with everything in this book. This book is a quest to find the truth. It's a journey.

Right from the time I was mature enough to think on my own, I wanted to achieve something big, tremendous, exciting, fascinating and mind-boggling. I just didn't know what that something was.

In my early childhood days, I wanted to become a bus driver when I grew up, while other children said that they wanted to become an engineer or a doctor. After a geography class in standard four, I developed a curiosity for space, earth, moon, stars and rockets that I wanted to be a scientist. In class five or six, I was incredibly spiritual and wanted to become a priest to serve God for the rest of my life. I felt like this till the day I saw the 'goddess' and fell in love with her.

In the filthy mess of life, she was an angel!

After high school, I took up science. On an impulse, I desired to be an airline pilot. But considering my personality, I soon realised that this wasn't a dream but a nightmare. Moving on, I switched desires to be a software engineer till the day I discovered the beauty of the animation industry and began nursing a desire to be an animator. I studied animation for three years and then worked for another three years. And then arose an itch in life. I was exhausted going to office and doing the same things, differently over and over again. It dawned on me that my life was stagnant. Then I got the concept for this book. For a while, I even toyed with the idea of writing the script for a movie with the concept.

Never in my life did I think I would one day become a writer. Writing is not in my DNA or genes, literally not in my jeans. I do not have much hands-on experience in writing. None of my relatives, friends or the people I know are writers. I do not have a godfather in this field. But destiny always catches up with you on the very road you try to avoid. I once had a random thought about writing a book but it faded away when I woke up the next morning. I want to tell you about this book: how it all began, how the idea came about and how it was conceived. I will try to explain everything in a few words and not drag on for too long.

I relentlessly thought of writing a book for over six months. I had all kinds of ideas for a book, but I would always keep coming back to this particular topic. It was stuck in my brain. I asked myself several times, "Is this the subject matter I want to opt for, that too for my first book? Am I mature and experienced enough to write about this?" I thought a lot. I pondered, wondered and read a lot about this particular topic. I observed people and talked to them a lot. After some time, I couldn't get the topic out of my head. I couldn't defer my decision on it. I never had the heart to change the topic. I thought that if I was ever going to write a book, this would be the subject I would put pen to paper on.

Bursting forth with ideas, my brain worked overtime. What if I failed? Would I be able to do it? *Maa, baap kya kehenge? Log kya kehenge? Society kya kehegi?* (What would my mother and father think? What would people think? What would society think?) I had all kinds of thoughts inspired from soap operas and TV serials. And I hadn't scribbled a single word yet! After days of procrastination, I knew the moment finally arrived when I started to write, not bothered about the consequences. I commenced. Then I began to think again. Where do I start? What do I write? How do I write? Who would read what I wrote? What is the first letter that would set everything in motion? I took a call. There were just twenty-six letters in the English alphabet. I just had to pick one. I told myself I could do it. I told myself that I would write just three pages of whatever came to my mind and take a call at the end of it. So I jumped off the cliff in a jiffy and realised I could fly too.

As I wrote those pages, the words started flowing. I was thrilled. I was charged. It just got better and better. I didn't stop with three pages. I wrote around twenty-five pages on the first day. I felt like the king of the world, born to write. I had a good first day and I was satisfied and happy. I had a comforting night's sleep.

The next day, I woke up and tried to carry forward the previous day's work. I sat for thirty minutes. Then forty-five minutes. I sat idle for an hour. Not a single word popped into my head. My genius writing ability of the previous day had vanished without any trace. In short, I was back! In the next twenty to twenty-five days, I managed to write forty to fifty pages.

Down the journey, I lost interest. I became lazy and clueless about what to write. I wasn't serious enough and I started losing motivation and confidence about making it. I thought the spark I had enjoyed in the first few days was just beginner's luck. I began to think that my destiny wasn't writing, that I had perhaps made a wrong call and it was yet another of my bad decisions.

For the next two or three months, I took a break from writing and spent a lot of time reading motivational quotes, inspirational articles, blogs, autobiographies and self-help books and watching videos. This led me back to writing. I began to take my book seriously and started writing with fervour. Soon enough, my fear of failure vanished. Of course, there were the occasional bouts of laziness, but I never gave up.

Here I am today achieving one of my wildest dreams – writing a book!

When I started writing this book, I didn't even know the exact format, where to start, how to continue and how to end the book. So, I devised my own format, my own way of telling a story and my own perspective on how a book should be. I wrote a lot more than what the final version has today. I also added a lot after completing the book, at the last minute.

Writing was fun; thinking was even more fun. I had a lot of fun writing this book – going on long walks, arguing, raising questions, finding answers, reading what I had written over again and again, dreaming, banging my head, feeling lazy, having sleepless nights, making excuses, postponing to the next day or sometimes the next week, worrying about the readers, publishing, sales, content, deleting the unnecessary drags, clearing confusions, feeling depressed, lost, lonely and frustrated and experiencing joy, contentment and thrill. It was one hell of a ride. I really loved the whole new magical experience writing a book gave me.

Now, a few months after completing this book, I don't want to settle for being just a writer. I want to be a best-selling author. I want this book to be read by millions of people across the planet. While writing and reviewing the book, I expanded my vision and thinking on a global scale. The content has been carefully chosen and perfected to the best of my ability. The language is simple and straight and easy for everyone to understand.

I was just another ordinary clown on the street with a big dream of writing a book. I set off on the path to becoming an extraordinary person. During the journey, I figured out that the difference between the ordinary and the extraordinary was that **little EXTRA!**

Why Should You Read this Book?

Are you a bookworm? Do you read novels, fiction, comics, romance, crime, thriller, suspense, detective, fantasy, spiritual, e-books, blogs, articles, magazines, textbooks or at least a newspaper?

Well, if you are not a big fan of reading, then this is the time and opportunity to start reading. This book is written with 'YOU' in mind. This is your story about your destiny. Now you may ask me how this is possible when I don't even know you. Read on to find out how. Usually in novels, the protagonist is the hero. In this book, you are the hero. This book is not just for someone or somebody. This book is for everyone and everybody who can read, understand and digest English, of course.

This book doesn't have any specific target audience. This book is not only for the working class men of the sub-Saharan region, who are married, under the age of thirty-three and a father of three kids. No, this book is for the entire humanity: teenagers, students, young, uncles, aunties, adults, old people and even the people nearing their end. This book is also for the future generation, which is not even born yet. I always wanted to write a book covering the entire mankind, irrespective of the continent, country, race, region, religion, caste, language, culture, tradition, belief and God.

Broadly, this book is meant for those above the age of eighteen. The reason is: eighteen is the age when a lot of things happen. At this age, we become mature enough to understand and make decisions on our own. We are not considered kids anymore. We begin to discern the good from the bad. We are eligible to choose our prime minister. Women can get married once they turn eighteen. There are certain topics in this book that will serve as Brett Lee's bouncers to children. So I would recommend this book for those eighteen and above.

Is this book funny, serious, informative or sentimental? What category does it fall under: drama, horror, thriller, happy ending, romance, reality, fantasy, fun-facts, war, sci-fi, future, fiction or non-fiction? Under which genre should the book fall in order to be successful? A book which is printed on the best-in-class paper? Is it a knowledgeable book or a book to pass your time? What is it? Unfortunately, this book doesn't fall under any of the above existing categories. This book is unique in a different way. I had to come up with a new category for "this book-**The Ultimate Category!"**

How does a book make everyone happy at the same time? How do I make someone buy this book? Is it all about how attractive the cover page is? Or how interesting the title is? Is it the summary on the back cover? The price? Is it the topic? What's the deciding factor that makes a book sail to success? How does one make the reader turn to the next page, making sure he reads every single word and every line, before he turns over the page? How does one ensure the reader is hooked till the last word on the last page of the book?

I haven't written a love story with a happy ending. This is not a story on mother-son sentiment, a heart melting *macchu-longu* story, a mathematical or a rocket science book. This book isn't a story or a novel. It is neither fiction nor non-fiction. It is not my autobiography and it is definitely not about pet animals.

I have put my heart, mind and soul in the process of creating this book. This book is about that **'one thing'** that is common to all the people who have ever lived on the surface of the earth, living right now and will take birth in the future, irrespective of gender, religion, caste, tradition, language, race, nationality, tribe, civilisation, economic status and education. This happens to animals, birds and the fishes too! It happens to you and me. Oh for god's sake, it's not love!

This thing happens to all of us. No one has ever escaped from it and nobody is ever going to. This book is about that durable truth, which everyone, including me, always chooses to FORGET! Those un-asked questions! But how far can we run from it? How many secrets can it hold? How many miracles can we handle? Some people laugh, a few people cry, but everybody has to be silent! If you have guessed what 'it' is, I admire your intelligence.

This book will definitely make you think, re-think and reclaim your life. It will have at the least a slight impact in your life, I am pretty sure about it. I may not be perfectly right in all that I have said, but I am not completely wrong either.

This book is extremely fabulous; you can trust me on this, because I myself have written it! LOL! You may think that every writer tells the same thing about his or her book. This book had an unexpected wallop on me. It revolutionised the way I think, live, understand and look at things and humanity all around. It didn't happen all of a sudden, but gradually. I hope it changes the way you think too.

I personally went to book stores and searched online, but I failed to find a single book like this, identical in terms of content, writing and the genre itself. So there is no competition or comparison with any other book. I am not proclaiming this to be the greatest book ever written, read and published. But I do believe it is one of a kind. You will acknowledge this when you finish reading the book.

A Mild Warning!

The titles of the chapters may sound a little eerie and sometimes spine-chilling and disturbing. Don't be afraid to read the chapters that reflect the tangible truth.

Each chapter deals with the ass-kicking truth and ear-splitting reality of life and its predictions. The content may sound offensive to a certain group of people or community. But this book isn't an attempt to hurt anyone's feelings in any way. The truth has to be spoken about at some point or the other. All readers may not be in harmony with the words written in this book. But the book brings out the truth from my perspective. Your version of truth may be different. As Swami Vivekananda said, "Truth can be stated in a thousand ways, yet each one could be true!" Everyone has their own identifiable reason, logic, understanding and beliefs about the same truth, in a thousand different ways. You don't have to agree with everything that is written in this book. Well, these are my thoughts. My truth. I mean no offence to anyone.

This book has the general global audience in mind. It isn't targeted at any particular person, group, community, religion or God. Read this book with a positive approach, an optimistic attitude and an open mind to experience its thrill. Do not take anything too personal. To be honest, there is no sentiment of any nature in this book. If you come across something sentimental at any point of time, control yourself and come out of your senti-mental feelings. It wasn't written to make you senti - mental.

If you want to judge this book (or for that matter any book or movie), you have to go through it completely. Half-knowledge is dangerous. Don't come to any conclusion without finishing the book. Questions, arguments, debates and queries will be entertained and considered valid only if you have completely read this book. My words may hurt you here and there. It all depends on how you are going to take the contents. I am certainly not forcing you to read this book. It is up to you to make the decision to read the book further.

The truth sets you free, but not before pissing you off.

Let's Get Started...

Thank you for your decision to read further and turning over the page. You have made a righteous decision. Congratulations! It means a lot to me. This means you are interested in knowing what I have to say. Well, let's get started then. I hope you have a good time reading this book. I hope the book gives you a whole new experience and do not regret having read it.

Lie back, take a big deep breath a couple of times and relax. Let your mind be clear from all the distractions of the world. Find a silent and a peaceful place to read. Don't let anybody or anything disturb you. If possible, keep your phone away or in silent mode. When reading, just focus on the words. Do not think about anything else. Do not multi-task. Take breaks, sleep if you feel like, but read the book with a fresh mind. Don't set any targets, read the book when you want to. Do not worry about what you are going to read because honestly even I didn't know what I was going to write ahead. Spend your valuable time on this book. Read this book with patience.

If you are looking for the contents page, then I am sorry. You won't find one. I feel the contents page spoils the fun and ruins the suspense about what you are going to read ahead. I don't know how it works in other books but then this isn't like any other book. In this particular book, I do not want to reveal the chapters. I want you to read this book page by page, chapter by chapter. The best is always preserved for the last. Do not skip anything and flip over the pages. Have a good sense of humour while reading it.

Write down any thoughts or questions you may have while reading this book. I would be delighted to know what you think and answer your queries.

HAPPY READING! ALL THE VERY BEST!

SEE YOU ON THE OTHER SIDE…

GO, no GO for the Launch…

- Booster.

- Go.

- Guidance.

- Guidance, go flight.

- Surgeon.

- Go Flight.

- Control.

- Go.

- Procedure.

- We are go.

- Network.

- Go.

- Recovery.

- We are go, Flight.

- Launch control, this is Houston.

We are Go for launch…

- Roger that, Houston! GOD, what's your status?

"We are GO for LAUNCH!"

T minus 60 seconds and counting…

T Minus Ten Seconds…

Nine………

Eight……..

Seven…….

Six……

Main engine starts…..

Three…

Two..

One.

Ignition!

We have a lift-off!

The End!

No one wants to die and yet death is the destination we all share. No one has ever escaped it. And this is as it should be, because death is very likely the best invention of life. It's the life's change agent. It clears out the old to make way for the new.

- Steve Jobs

Once upon a time in the Far East, there lived a king whose sovereignty was twice as big as India in terms of its size. The king had a huge defence force consisting of 25,512 well-trained soldiers, 45,333 horses, 15,716 elephants, modern ammunition and tenacious commanders. He built a mammoth 100-feet statuesque confine wall around his empire, protecting it from the immediate attack of his enemies. He looked after his citizens well, fed them sufficiently during famine and didn't accumulate taxes. The residents of his kingdom were free to do whatever they wanted.The king didn't cause them any inconvenience.

The king's only weakness was women. He had seventeen beautiful queens, thirteen mistresses, nine girlfriends and forty-one naughty children. He still didn't seem to be satisfied. He was lustful for more. His majesty's court was teeming with Bharatanatyam dancers, classical singers, storytellers, poets and painters, and all of them were women. The king, when overwhelmed with their works, rewarded them with gold coins, glittering jewellery and white sparkling pearls and even made them his own.

The educated astrologers of his kingdom warned the king that if he continued his half-witted senseless behaviour…

Did you think my book would begin like this? With a classic cheesy clichéd tale that happened once upon a time? Certainly not!

It launches like this…

My beloved ladies and gentlemen, let us begin from the stars. Do you know what is in common to Adam, Eve, Albert Einstein, Adolf Hitler, Swami Vivekananda, Indira Gandhi, Mother Teresa, Michael Jackson, Kalpana Chawla, Steve Jobs and Dr APJ Abdul Kalam? Yes, you guessed it right. They all are dead and far gone, with no sign of them ever coming back.

A for apple, B for ball, C for cat and D for? What if you don't wake up alive tomorrow morning? Do you know which good night is your last one? Where is everybody's life ultimately heading to? What is our final destination? How different will your death be from mine or the others? What is in the distant future is all the same. Death! Be happy that you are still alive and kicking and reading this.

Try to be alive every moment. You will anyway die someday. Yes, eventually all of us die. So let's face the solitary hard-naked truth of life. What is our moment of truth? How is it all going to end? Will it be a safe and sound happy ending as shown in the movies? *And they lived happily ever after…*Who is to be blamed for causing our death? Is it the flesh and blood's unstoppable destiny? What is death? Can it be fixed so that we can veritably prevent people from dying? Can we use cutting-edge technology to stop death? Is that even possible? Well, theory says it is possible.

Or does it? Our life has turned out like this these days. The first half of our life is spent pleasing our parents and the second half of our vital spark is spent pleasing our spouse and children. When do we live for our ownselves? Shouldn't we be able to live our own life? How long can we sacrifice our lives for the sake of others and fulfill others' dreams and desires? Have we ever thought about this? Do we know that the life we are living today is going to end in a blackout some day? Are we geared up for everything that is approaching our boulevard?

What happens after we rest in peace? Is death at a higher plane than life? Is death a promotion to the next level? Is it better than earthly life? Do eternity and heaven exist unceasingly as we believe them to? As we were promised? Can we know all the answers before we vanish? If yes, who is going to answer all these questions: people, religion or God?

Everyone knows that everybody is going to fade away someday, but people don't want to think or talk about it. Can our ignorance make us live forever? The older we get, the closer we are to paradise. Life is all about staying alive; everything else is secondary, regardless of how expensive and valuable it is. Nothing else in the entire universe can be more important to us than our own life. We may have all the money, power and resources to buy every little and big thing in the world, but we need to stay alive in order to enjoy the thrill of what we buy. What is the point of having the whole caboodle if we are not alive to experience it?

Do you know that ninety-five per cent of people who have ever lived on this planet earth are dead? Yes, you read it right. We are all here for a very limited period of time. We have to 'live here' and beyond a shadow of doubt 'leave from here' someday. We just don't know when that fine day will come. We not only live once, but we also die just once.

We all depart from this life but we do not know when, where, how and why? Death is obvious. No one can prosper forever. You can't live till the birds come home. But people rarely talk about termination. Everyone is terror-stricken about death. But no matter what we think, say, not say, what we did and where are we from, there is no escape from death. Who can give us the option to escape death? Can God give us that goddamn option? Why would He? Just because we were sincere in our prayers, went to the temple, mosque or church often and offered plenty of sacrifices to Him? No. Eternal rest does not need our permission. It doesn't need an approval or a signature from the divine power himself.

Life is a big one-time opportunity. Every single sunrise gives us a new hope, a fresh opportunity to change our life, to live life in respectable liveliness, achieve all our dreams and worship what we love doing. Death is a full stop to all our excuses for not leading a full life. Once dead, there is absolutely no today, tomorrow or weekend. Death is a full-time job, with no breaks, weekly offs, sick leaves, national holidays and vacations. Fatality is more complicated than a woman's mind. Death isn't recyclable. It isn't just the end; it is the end of all ends from every end. THE END of every single fuckin' thing!

Our earth is 4.55 billion years old. It has extremely limited resources and a fragile environment. The population on earth has rapidly risen in the past 200 years. We were a population of one billion in 1820, two billion in 1930, three billion in 1960, four billion in 1974, five billion in 1988 and six billion in 2000. The earth's population today is 7.3 billion people and counting.

Even after the invention of condoms and contraceptive pills, our population is so huge. Just imagine a world without them. I guess even the planet Mars would have been overcrowded by now.

Coming back to the earth, with this rate of rise in population, by 2020 or at the most 2025, we may even reach eight billion. There is approximately one death to every three births. Every second, approximately five people are born and two are dead at any given instance of time around the world. About 100 people expire every minute, 6,000 perish every hour, 1,50,000 die every day and about 60 million breathe their last every year. But each year, 70–75 million people are added on earth. The overall population on earth is growing and growing!

To begin with, let's not be disheartened by death. It is a beautiful and complicated truth. One should never be suspicious of the truth. Nevertheless, we are still anxious about this truth. Downfall is certain. We don't have the power to ignore, reject, change or hide from it. We are in no position to give any excuse to death. We cannot tell death that we are in a bad mood, we are not ready for it, we need more time, we have some unfinished business to take care of or it is too early. We cannot even buy time saying we need to take a shower before death dawns on us.

Relax! Talking and reading about death definitely doesn't lead you die. Seeing will not cost you, buying will. We don't die if we 'see' poison; we die only if we consume it.

There are millions of ways to kick the bucket. The basic categories are: natural ageing, deadly disease, natural calamity, accident, murder and suicide. Funerary may not exactly be our friend; however, it is not our enemy too. Death is mandatory, whether we like it or not. I keep repeating this word and harping on this truth, because we need to understand it completely and unmistakably. Death doesn't give a damn to what we think, how frightened we are, how much we hate it and ignore it. Death is honest. It knows no discrimination. It doesn't mislead us and make any fake promises. It doesn't give jaw-dropping discounts or make manipulating advertisements. It makes us rest in peace. Oh boy! Hasn't humanity been long fighting for peace?

Everybody can fight, but honestly nobody is going to win over it. Do you want to compete with it? Go ahead. Nothing is stopping you, not even death. Our cooking oil may be cholesterol-free, but we still have to pay for oil. But in death, we don't have to pay a penny for the service. There are no taxes, advanced booking, caste-based reservation, service charge, tips or finder's fee. Death comes with no strings attached and zero terms and conditions. It doesn't accept any bribe – so corruption-free. We don't need an agent or a broker to deal with it. We can and have to encounter it on our own - savings on brokerage. It doesn't demand anything from us, except our life. And come on, you always knew that you would definitely die someday. It's not that I am enlightening you today.

Well, all that I said was supposed to make you less terrified about death. Is it working? Truth be told, it doesn't make a difference how melodiously I narrate this or how much I sugarcoat it, the corporeality is unaffected.

Nothing will change. It is still DEATH! Relax. Take a chill pill! There is a lot of kick in talking about a kickass topic such as death.

Figuratively speaking, we are blind-dating death at all times. She resides next to us always, she walks hand in hand with us and even sleeps with us without making a sound. If she wakes up, we sleep for eternity. When she reveals herself, will we be able to meet, feel and experience her for a nanosecond? Or everything will be over in a flash - JUST LIKE THAT! The sad thing is we can date her only once. Where are we going to hide when she comes for us? She has several creative ways to surprise us and entertain us. Instead of being pessimistic and worrying about death, let's try to understand it. Let us Un-CoMpLiCaTe it.

May be we don't want to die, and we certainly don't ask for it, but she will come and find us. She will catch us. What is the point of being dramatic and sentimental about her then? She doesn't spare anyone. Does death knows every last one of us by name? Where do the dead people go? Is death the answer to all of our questions?

You knew this all along, didn't you? It's time to be aware of death, accept it, explore it, deal with it and not be panic-stricken about it. Learn to respect it, because you clearly cannot stop it. We live today to die another day.

Death – The End!

Are you faint-hearted to read ahead about death? If yes, trust me, by the end of this book, you won't be. If no, that's fantastic. Either way, just continue reading.

Stage 2
Death is for Everyone!

In the long run, we all are dead.

- John Keynes

Well, let me be honest: Death is for everyone. You are not the first and you are definitely not the last. You are not the only victim. You may read this book from top to toe or not. You may not be curious or you may feel sleepy reading this book. Well, that doesn't stop you from dying. The truth is: this book is about the facts, figures, mysteries, truths, beliefs and assumptions encircling death, but it is not simply in favour of death. There is more. It may sound creepy, interesting, weird, or scary. However you take it, it doesn't make any difference.

Death isn't racist. It embraces everybody in the same way. You, me, he, she, him, her, it, father, mother, brother, sister, husband, wife, married, divorced, children, cousin, single, engaged, boyfriend, girlfriend, ridiculous, rascal, liar, smoker, drunkard, doper, banker, online shopper, magician, pilgrimage, white, black, Japanese, Chinese, American, Australian, African, Indian, Tamilian, Russian or Asian. It is for everyone and for every fuckin' body!

It doesn't matter whether you are a dude, bro, babe, NASA scientist, stranger, neighbour, child, unemployed, weak, healthy, a mistake, lazy, hungry, sick, in love, heartbroken, minor, widow, racist, war hero, humble, honest, billionaire, homeless, struggling model, porn star, animator, engineer, photographer, psychologist, successful, loser, stupid, beautiful, short-tempered, loved by all, accused, murderer, writer, patient, or a doctor. Further down the pyramid of life, death is also for the dog, cat, pig, lion, giraffe, snake, crow, eagle, peacock, penguin, shark, dolphin, starfish, frog, crocodile, housefly, ant, cockroach, lizard, mosquito, bacteria, tomato plant, mango tree, money plant, rose plant, algae and alien. Anything that crawls, walks, runs, moves, flies, sleeps and swims DIES!

Death is for all; there is no religion or caste barrier. It is for the Christian, Hindu, Muslim, Buddhist, Jain, Sikh, Jew, Roman Catholic, Brahmin, D'Souza, Reddy, Gowda, Shia, Rajput, Pinto, Yadav, Gupta, Lobo, Pandey, Protestant and Sunni. It is mandatory even for the Prime Minister of India, the President of the United States of America, the Queen of England, the King of Saudi Arabia and the dictators of West Asia. Nothing really matters. No babe! Not at all, death never minds. NEVER!

It is physically, chemically, biologically, electronically, theoretically, experimentally, scientifically, mentally, spiritually, religiously, blindly, honestly, proudly, legally, illegally, practically and accidentally impossible to stop death.

Death has nothing to do with anything. It doesn't have to ask our permission or send us random clues before its arrival. But there are instances and recorded cases where death did give big clues before its arrival. But are we so developed to understand, plan and react to its arrival? For more information on this, watch the *Final Destination* movie series.

Death doesn't directly send us a formal mail, give a 'missed' call or leave a text message before its arrival. Sometimes, ailing patients suffering deadly diseases know they are going to die soon. But they too don't know exactly when and how specifically it's all going to end. Death isn't a mystery, it is the truth. Is death really the end of life or is it the beginning of something new?

There are so many gods in heaven or maybe there is just one and we refer to Him by different names. Wells, ponds, streams, reservoirs, lakes, rivers and seas are called by different names, but they all contain the same thing: water. They may flow through different parts of the world but ultimately they join the same big ocean of the earth.

Yet human beings cannot digest the fact that He is one. Just one. Fine, it's not a problem whether there is just one or too many, because no matter how many gods are actually out there or how many gods we have created ourselves, none of the gods can save us from dying. This is the truth, the actual fact. This is the way it is supposed to be and this is the way exactly it is. Death is independent of all parameters, sources, internal and external factors. Nothing can come in its way. Death is powerful. It may be a miracle. It may be the most beautiful thing that humanity will ever encounter in its lifetime. (After its lifetime, to be specific.) Who knows? No one who has seen it is alive to tell the story. Death is for everyone, everybody and every single living thing on earth. It doesn't matter whether you are interested or not. If there is life, then there is death too for sure. Don't worry, everyone dies eventually!

Stage 3
In Death, We Become Almost Everything

Death solves all the problems – no man, no problems.

- Joseph Stalin

One moment, we are breathing and in the next split second we are dead. We become almost everything. We become blind, deaf, dumb, heartbroken, our kidneys don't function, we are not hungry or thirsty. There is no urine, no sweat, no shit. The body is completely dehydrated; there is no pulse, heartbeat, brain function, blood circulation or the senses of touch and feel. We cannot nod our head or sniff our own rotting body. We can't even remember to forget or breathe to prove that we are alive. There is no hangover of life. The solicitation is over in the twinkling of an eye, everything passes in a flash. KABOOOM!

Unfortunately, there is no room for loneliness. We are doomed to be on our own. No one is going to stretch a helping hand. There is no family, well-wishers, friends, boyfriends, girlfriends, spouse, children and not even enemies. We are all alone till hell freezes over. Who has even the slightest conception about how long death is going to last? We know we can live a maximum of 100 years, but how long are we dead?

Once in the throes of death, we cannot take a selfie, send a text message, update status on Facebook or WhatsApp, tweet, check in, do a Google search, watch a YouTube video, send an e-mail, watch porn, waste our time, get busy, go on a holiday, enjoy the weekend at a graveyard twilight party all night long, earn or spend money, crawl, sit, stand, kneel, walk, run, drive, swim, smile, laugh, giggle, lie, do crazy stuff, smoke, booze, dope, masturbate, apply make-up, dress up cool, eat pizzas, burgers, ice-cream or chocolate, make peace, listen to our favourite music or go for a movie. There is no more first-day-first-show as our last-day-last-show is over. We cannot try to be bold and confident, give an interview or apply for banking exams; we cannot vote, wonder why 'it' happened to us or ask *why me*?

Well, with death, everybody gets a chance. It is just a question of time. Today it is theirs, tomorrow it's ours. We are all standing in the same long queue waiting for our turn. Our flight's origin, class (business or economy) and altitude maybe different, but the destination is one and the same. If life is a 'journey,' then death is the 'destination.'

All the people who attended our funeral would have driven back home by now, leaving us behind, all by ourselves. How many of them ought to still cry for us? They all have better things to think, do and fix. Moreover, they have their own lives to worry about. The earth is not going to stop rotating, the dogs don't quit barking or the planes don't nosedive from the skies, just because we are dead. In the outside world, practically nothing changes.

Our insurance nominees get busy processing our death certificate and executing the formalities and documentation of our insurance policy. They may be battling with the insurance company regarding the tax deduction on the insurance money. Our nominees may have expected a lavish fortune and the insurance company may not be giving it to them. When we die, the insurance premium money that we faithfully paid every year without fail, like a good boy is valued over and above us.

Yes, there are a handful of people who will genuinely mourn our death, miss us, remember us and cry for us. But how many people do this? And for how many days? They will cry for a few days and then move on. Today, tomorrow, a week from now or a year later. You may have also in your lifetime attended funerals. At how many funerals did you really mourn? You may have lost people beloved to you. For how many days did you cry and remember them? One day? Two days? A week? A month? A whole year? What happened after that?

Have you sincerely observed the individuals attending a funeral? If not, then do it the next time. Study them, notice their actions, scan their eyes and see how they behave just ten to fifteen minutes after the funeral. Homo sapiens tend to forget the fact that they just attended a funeral. I have seen this almost at every funeral I have been to.

We can unmistakably identify who is genuinely grief-stricken and who is faking it. We can also come across jokers who try hard to control their laughter. These people give a little peek into what will happen at your own funeral.

The sun rises and gives light and energy to the earth, the earth rotates and revolves around the sun, the birds sing, the wind blows, water evaporates, clouds are formed, it rains, rivers flow, crops grow, people are born, they live, get educated, go to work, start new business, build skyscrapers touching the skies, make money, commit sins, get married, have kids, get older, accidents happen, people die, movies get released, there is summer, winter, monsoon and autumn seasons and the sunsets. Life moves on, with us or without us.

Back to becoming everything, we just cannot complain, blame, raise queries, shoot questions, give our valuable feedback and suggestions or call up customer care to express our uneasiness concerning death. We can't even send a formal mail to God. Assuming that the God of Death, Yamaraj, picks your call, what will you complain about? Would you tell him that you are feeling very lonely, bored, scared, dark and dead and that there is barely any fun and hardly any entertainment to kill time?

The terribly sickening scenario once we are breathless is this: nobody fancies calling us by our name anymore. We all attain a universally accepted well-known name: BODY. The living beings refer to us as the 'body.' Bring the body here, send the body for post-mortem, lower the body, bury the body, burn the body. Where did our elegant and angelic name disappear? The name with which we were called by all of our lifetime. Were we not trying to impress people all our lives with our name? We were so obsessed with it and honoured by it. But we relinquish our name once we are dead.

So make sure you earn wings and flying colours, do something noble, render service for the betterment of the community, society, country or the world. So that, even if you surrender your name to death, at least you don't kiss goodbye to your identity. Do something useful to society or come up with innovative solutions to the hitches and glitches of life, so that people remember you even after your demise. Everyone is born ordinary, but make sure you don't live a routine mediocre life and have a meaningless monotonous death.

Nobody, not a single soul, can save us. None of the gods in heaven is going to descend and rescue us from the process of dying. Are you 100 per cent goddamn sure of the bliss in heaven and eternity? Not a single person alive has ever experienced it. We haven't found any meticulous scientific evidence regarding these hallucinating fantasies. Are we in some sort of sym-'pathetic' blinded superstitious belief?

They say that God has enough talent, resources, magical powers, supremacy and the authority to raise us back from the dead. Well, that does sound promising. But why would He simply do that? As an introductory limited period offer, because we are dying for the first time? Would He do that to impress us? To prove that He is capable of doing it? What great deed can we do to impress the Divine so that He calls us from death? God cannot just pick a random person and give him or her life back. That would be considered injustice, right? Are there any instances or at least rumours of such a thing happening? Not 2,000, 5,000 years or 10,000 years ago! Have there been any recorded incidents of late? What about 10, 20, 50, 100, 500 or at least 1000 years ago? All the gods stopped visiting the earth a long time ago! With no recent noticeable actions, gods are part of history now. Even if we assume that God managed to bring a few back from the dead, what are they going to be called? Ghosts?

Stage 4
The Past Tense

Everything that gets born, dies.

- Morrie Schwartz

Death is the reality, but it is not a reality TV show. It is pure, transparent, mysterious and magical. It is like a stranger waiting at the tail end of life. We can't stay here on earth forever. We all have to leave the earth someday, making way for the younger, better and faster generations to come. But before we die, we have to make sure that we leave this planet a better place than what we were put into. A better place for mankind, animals, plants and even marine life.

Second by second minutes pass, minute by minute hours pass, hour by hour days pass, day by day weeks pass, week by week months pass, month by month years pass, year by year life passes by. Life moves at a snail's pace, and is turned into death and then life is shut down forever, as if it never existed! Is there a restart? We don't know. We can only cross our fingers, hope for the best, wish ourselves good luck and pat our own backs.

Our routine way of living with an established timetable, our lifestyles, habits, tastes and our physical body change once we are dead. Death is a transformation, the ultimate change. There are no more alterations. And this change happens only once. Once we are dead, everything echoes into the past tense. The life that we lived until yesterday is the past. So let's call it the past tense. The life that we are living today is a gift, which is why it is called the present. Life now is the present tense. The life that we are going to live ahead is the future. That is the future tense.

If we're dead, all we can think of is this (though I don't know if we can think once we are dead): yeah, I once had a family, relatives, friends and girlfriends. I once owned an expensive luxury car and a big bungalow. I was once married, I had kids. I lied, lied all the time. I was always Mr Late and now I am Late Mr. I once lived, I once had a life.

Everything switches to the past tense once we are dead.

We are going to be the past, not the future, once we are dead. Nobody uses our name or anything related to us in the present tense. Everyone is going to refer us is in the past tense. He CAME to my place last evening. We HAD a conversation over the phone this morning. He WAS a good person. We MADE plans for meeting up tomorrow, he SAID he wanted to talk to me about something very important and he WAS very excited about it. *Par ye raaz bhi usi ke saath chala gaya* (the secret went away with him). He SENT a text message an hour before he died, but I was a bit busy to reply to him. She WOKE up early this morning. She WAS very silent all day long. She didn't even have breakfast. We thought she would make it for another month or two, but she died all of a SUDDEN.

All we are left with is the past. Our past life that we have left behind, which consisted of many people, several memories, the money that we made, the way we lived our life, the things that we believed in, the God (or god's) we worshipped, the sacrifices we made, the community service we did and the good and the bad we did to others and to our self – everything is in the past. How much did we live for ourselves? Did we make the one-time adventure ride called life worth living? Do we have the power to remember all our memories and think about our past life once dead? Neither our brain nor any other part of our body will remind us of our black and white memories. Because we are just dead meat now! "When we're alive: Death is 'future guaranteed tense' and once we're dead, death becomes 'the past tense.'"

Stage 5
Death Doesn't Care How Rich We Are

In this world nothing can be said to be certain,
except taxes and death.

- Benjamin Franklin

Oh yeah, baby! Death isn't xenophobic to discriminate the living entities on any basis. Death happens regardless of how educated, rich, intelligent, brilliant, accurate, clear, honest, famous or good a person 'is,' in the long haul of life will definitely going to be 'was'. We may have billions of dollars that may give us a good life, better food, more freedom, consistent happiness, sustainable success, expensive cars, big houses, and chartered flights. We may get treated by the world's best doctor at the world's top ranked hospital. All those surgeries, medicines, machines, technology, tests and lab results may postpone our death by a few years. But what happens next?

No matter how much money we have, we cannot obstruct the process of dying. Death doesn't come with an EMI option, fancy discounts, cash back offers, coupons, bonus, buyback guarantee, or warranty. Death maybe just another routine inspection, like an oil change.

We cannot cough up money to be liberated. We don't get a tiny signature to escape death. Our credit cards won't be accepted at the ticket counters of the graveyard. What is the cost of one ticket? Is there a return ticket? Are the food and the drinks free of cost, healthy and tasty on the ride back to our original home from where we came? Is God waiting for us to come home? Who wants to go to heaven? Who doesn't? How far are the gates of heaven from hell? Is there a shorter route to heaven? Where is death taking us? To the stars?

Death is for every single person: the person sitting right next to you, colleagues in office, well-wishers, enemies, salesmen and strangers you have never seen in your life. Everyone is going to die. We can run, but we cannot hide. There is no known, easy, reliable, safe, straight, and promised escape.

Let's talk some sense here. Our life is a mess in general. We have successful business, good contacts, recommendations, priorities, fame, money, respect, gratitude, madness, anxiety and expectations. Unsatisfied with all this, we go in search of more, leading a battle. We steer the ship that has reached the middle of the deep ocean onto the shores of the destined land on the other side, across the mighty long waves. We overcome sharks, deep waters, strong rains, icebergs, violent weather, thunderstorms, lightning, pirates, spells of silent, calm and still waters. We also manage to escape from the Titanic and other ships that are sinking. We want to survive. We are powerful and purpose-driven. Amid all the mess, we somehow reach half the distance. We come across ups and downs, trials, errors, failures, successes, mistakes and experiences. We are educated. We can read, write, understand, analyse, think, judge and decide. We have common sense and we are open-minded.

We are not blind, deaf, dumb, physically challenged or hungry. We are not stupid. We are aware.

The humanity has money, gold, property, cars, shares, assets, religion, God, idols, technology, internet, computers, weapons, nuclear energy, atomic bombs, brains, logical-reasoning, judgment and thoughts. Our tiny inner voices constantly tell us what is right and what is not, what to do or not to do. These voices keep us civilised and in control. They protect us and guide us to the light and the shore. But our beliefs and half-knowledge have gone so viral, deep down inside us, into our saliva, haemoglobin, nucleus of our cells, tissues, DNA, genes, nerves, flesh, muscles, bones, vitamins, proteins, oxygen, sugars and salts, that we reach a place where we believe that, this is the truth that our inner voices have been telling us for days, weeks, months, years, decades and centuries. They don't appreciate the questions as they are the creator, the source of all rules, regulations, terms, conditions, taxes, hope, economic crises, rise in price of basic commodities, nightmares, democracy, promises, hopes and sentiments.

Once we are dead, the money that we earned all our life groans in the bank lockers. We are left with nothing, whether we are going to heaven or hell. It is not necessary where we're going and what we are going to do once we get there, but what are we even left with? Can we pack all our stuff neatly and carry it with us?

Death is not for sale. We cannot buy it. It is priceless. Our God, religion, spirituality, beliefs, faiths, sacrifices, visits to the church, temple and mosques, achievements, fears, ancestors, society, leaders, family, traditions, culture, job, health conditions, retirement, money, power, wealth, status, property, land, gold and women, none of this can buy death. What do you want to do? Where are you? Look at the world outside, it's alive. The earth is rotating and revolving around the sun at a speed of thirty kilometres per second.

No matter how light-skinned we are, we still need light in the dark. In spite of how tall we are, we cannot see tomorrow. Regardless of how rich we are and how many cars we have, we will always have to walk to the toilet. No matter how big and strong we are, we cannot carry ourselves to the grave. Life is awfully short. Take it easy.

Nothing is going to be ours anymore. We cannot take any of our things with us, we have to leave everything behind and go empty-handed. We didn't bring anything with us when we were born, similarly we cannot take anything with us when we leave. All the earthly things belong to the earth. We don't own properties; we just have our names temporarily on the documents.

If God is really out there, what is He doing? Is He busy watching us all the time? Is He listening to our never-ending loud prayers and demands? People on earth are making money in the name of God, religion, education, health care, tradition, name, culture, trademark, superstitious beliefs and so on. Superstitious belief is like searching for a black cat in a pitch-dark and profoundly silent room when you are blindfolded and finding the cat that isn't there. There is no point at all. We are afraid of the answers so much that we don't even want to ask the questions. What have we done to the world? Is God watching us all from 33,000 feet above the earth, hiding beneath the clouds of half-promises and unseen miracles? Does He know that we exist? We pray in all directions—north and south, east and west. Are our prayers successfully reaching Him on time?

When death knocks on our life's door, all we can do is surrender ourselves and everything to it. Do we have a choice? Who can we yell at? Who can we get angry at? Can we ask questions? What if we have any doubts? We may have an engineering degree or any other degree from the world's best university. We may work in Apple or Microsoft, we may be a businessman or a billionaire. But in our next life, no matter what we have done in our previous life, who, where and how we were, we have to start all over again from ZERO! We have to stay in our mother's womb for nine months, take birth and eventually learn to crawl, walk, sit, stand and talk all over again. Then we have to go to kindergarten, primary school, secondary school and high school, finish college, get a degree, a master's degree and a job, and then get married, have children, grow old, retire and finally die. It all ends up in different ways, but at the same point, stage and level. We have to deal with it.

We have to start over from the basics of the beginning. No matter what we owned in our previous life, it's going to end with our previous life. We won't even remember who or what we were in our past life. The experiences of our present life are not going to be accounted for in our next life. We have to start our new life as a fresher. Money may buy anything and everything in the world, including happiness and love. But no matter how much money we have, we cannot spend a single penny once we are dead. The one and the only one thing that money cannot buy is: life from the hands of death. Death doesn't really care how rich we are!

Stage 6
We Cannot Cheat Death

As a well-spent day brings happy sleep,
so a life well-spent brings happy death.

- Leonardo da Vinci

Death can be defined as "a little brown girl with black hair, very messy, lots of knots, and she doesn't like to brush it." That's okay! In the eyes of death, all living beings are identical. She is the final curtain of all arguments, debates, connections, fights, questions, answers and judgments. She is the final verdict. We cannot play games, create the rules, and dominate her. She accepts no bribe, unlike many government officials of India. We cannot just give money under the coffin and expect our work to be done. No, she doesn't accept any gifts, 'token advance,' reservation, or recommendation.

No matter who we are, whether we were born to someone or adopted, by choice or by mistake, whether we are good or bad, male or female, happy or angry, crawling or flying, young or old, silent or violent, loved or hated, smart or ridiculous, a vegetarian or a non-vegetarian, beautiful or ugly, white or black, gay or lesbian, pre-paid or post-paid, virgin or not, bachelor or married, family type or not, a saint or sinner, Hindu, Muslim or Christian, a servant or king, a boss or an employee, committed or single, a babe or a bitch, a tourist or a terrorist, a patient or a doctor, a child of someone famous, a father of three kids, not ready to die yet, still in the womb, just born, three months old, one year old, two years old, flora or fauna, domestic or wild, nothing matters in her eyes.

Death is spectacular, she is transparent. She may be the sexiest thing around. She is a feeling humanity will never encounter more than once.

If the sun has risen again, if we are alive today, we have another day to live, a new day to hope, a new chance to live our life better than yesterday and to love and be happy. Many millions of people didn't wake up today; they were all dead by yesterday. They neither have today nor tomorrow. Tens of people are literally dying outside in the world, as you are reading this. Another hundreds of people won't make it by the time you finish reading this page, thousands will be gone by the time you end this chapter and millions of people will be dead by the time you complete reading this book.

Take a chill pill. We can't stand do anything about her or stop her from coming to catch us. Yeah, even I wish I could stop her, but I cannot and no one can. So there is no use planning to rebel against her. We ultimately have to surrender ourselves to her when she conquers us. There is no other choice. If there is something that is really impossible, it is conquering death. All the other things in this world may be possible to do.

Many people try to avoid death or postpone it through exercises, yoga, meditation, Ayurvedic medicines, dieting and eating healthy food that is less in cholesterol, low on calories and sugar. People who have ailments undergo kidney dialysis or replacement of body parts such as kidney, liver and heart too. People are admitted in the intensive care unit for a very long period of time. They are in coma for long. But how long can they cheat death? Forever? All they can do is postpone death by a few days, weeks, months or at the most a few years. What happens after that?

Death does not compromise. She shows no mercy and sympathy. She has no heart, love, emotion or sentiment of any kind. Though it is ultimately going to be the same for everyone, the way each one dies is of course different.

Many people are dying from heart attacks these days. In ancient times, thousands of people died during war and epidemic diseases. More than sixteen million were killed in World War I alone and another sixty million in World War II.

People can die in several ways: accidents, natural death due to ageing, suicides, terrorist attacks, murder, sickness, unknown virus, AIDS, cancer, lack of hygiene, stroke, brain damage, dehydration, kidney failure, incorrect diagnosis, wrong medication, obesity, very low blood cell levels, sugar, diabetes, blood pressure, polio, malaria, bird flu, overdose of medicines, abortion, doctor's mistake, improper care, food poisoning, contaminated water, flood, famine, global warming, sunstroke, bomb blast, plane crash, depression, starvation, death in deep sleep, ignorance, smoking, drinking, drugs, reckless driving, drunken driving, sleeping on the footpath, being at the wrong place at the wrong time, snake bite, pollution, electric shock, phobia, concussion, storm, earthquake, heavy rain, lightning, hurricane, tsunami, hanged to death, assassination, mysterious reasons, poisonous gases, gas cylinder explosion, ambulance struck in traffic jam, forest fire, electromagnetic radiation, drowning, or when didn't know how to swim, adventures and kicks or as simple as while crossing the road. Literally anything can kill us, anywhere, at any time. We never know. We cannot guess, assume, or predict when and how she will get us. Are we ready for her surprise?

People may not like to die. They may hate death, ignore her and not want to think, read and understand death. For how many years do they want to live? 200 years? We can cheat on our boyfriend or girlfriend, spouse, friends, enemies or business partners. We can cheat the government by not paying tax or cheat the immigration officer. We can cheat ourselves by not marrying the person we love or by not following our dreams. But the only thing we cannot cheat or defy is death. We have absolutely no control over death. How can we convince her not to harm us? How can we convince her to allow us to live forever? What on earth can we give in return? Money, property, gold, diamond, shares or a Ferrari car? Death isn't greedy; she is not in need of anything, she has got everything. Everybody dies, but not everybody lives.

Stage 7
Self-Service!

Swapnil Chandrakanth (2nd year mechanical engineering, IIT Kanpur), G. Suman (2nd year, M. Tech, IIT Kanpur,) Vijay Nakula (4th year, CSE, IIT Powai), Abhilash J.J. (PhD, IIT Kanpur), Prashanth Kumar (1st year electrical engineering, IIT Kanpur), Anjan Kumar (2nd year chemical engineering, IIT Kanpur). Who are all these students? You may think they are the students who had done marvellous work in their respective fields, as they all are from the most prestigious colleges of India. No! These are the students who committed suicide unfortunately. Yes, suicide. You read it right.

These are the students who were under the tremendous pressure of marks, ranks, campus placements and humongous career opportunities from their parents, relatives and friends. They were considered the finest students in the country. But sometimes, the pressure of competition, studies, exams, projects, failures and campus placements make students lose control, their hope and confidence, leading them to commit suicide.

The word 'suicide' comes from the Latin word 'suicidism,' which means 'to kill oneself.' Suicide is defined as the intentional act of causing one's own death. The common reasons for suicide include financial crisis, fear of failure, frustration, depression, extreme stress, love failure, problems in relationship, loss of a family member or a friend, job, mental disorders, personality disorders, psychological disorders, sexual abuse, recent crisis, hopelessness, loneliness, health issues, drugs, insults, poverty, not finding a reason to live, silly reasons and so on.

In the US, a fourteen-year-old boy, the son of a lawyer, committed suicide by putting a bullet into his brain using his dad's revolver. The reason? His father had seized his phone and deactivated his Facebook account. The boy was found dead in his room the following morning. Where is the world heading?

There are several ways to commit suicide: hanging, sleeping pills, high dose medication, poison, pesticide, drug overdose, driving into accidents, shooting oneself, drowning, jumping from a mountain, building and so on. Suicide is considered to be the top fifteenth reason for death.

According to statistics, men are three to four times more the victims of suicide than women. Suicides resulted in 8,42,000 deaths worldwide in 2014 alone. The number of suicides has been increasing year on year, up from 7,12,000 deaths in 1990.These are the numbers from reported cases, the cases that have come to light. There are around ten to twenty million non-fatal suicide attempts made each year, which result in injuries. The victims are mostly young people, especially women. According to a research, every forty seconds someone commits suicide!

Over 2,00,000 farmers have committed suicide in India alone since 1997. The main reasons are poverty, debt, lack of rain and not getting the right price for their yield. These farmers were left with no other option but to commit suicide, leaving behind a lot of debt, which their wives and children have to repay. If the family too cannot repay it, what are they supposed to do? Commit suicide?

The rules, legalities and punishments for suicide are different in different parts of the world. In some countries it is illegal to commit suicide, while in other countries it isn't. But if the victim fails in his attempt to commit suicide, he is caught by the law. The victim is liable to penalties. In some countries, the people who failed to prevent the victim from committing suicide are also liable for punishment. It is considered illegal to support, force and manipulate anyone to commit suicide. In ancient Greek, suicides weren't accepted. The people who committed suicide were buried alone, separately in the outskirts of the city. But today, in most western countries, suicide is no longer a crime.

Mass suicide is a process by which several people commit suicide at once for a common cause. The highest number of people who committed suicide all at once was recorded in the year 1978 by the Peoples Temple, an American religious group led by Jim Jones, which resulted in the death of 918 people. Cyanide was mixed in grape wine and the people who drank the wine were made to believe that God was waiting for them in heaven. Are those 918 people in the seven-star executive rooms of heaven now?

When a man is suicidal, he thinks suicide is the ultimate solution for all the problems in the world. He feels all his master plans have failed and God has closed His eyes upon him. Maybe he expected way too much and kept thinking about his problems and past life so much that he failed to figure out a solution. This over time probably let him to depression.

People with suicidal tendencies take insults, criticism, mental torture, blackmail, business loss and love failures extremely serious that their life goes out of their control. They feel the only control they have is over their death. They think they have the right to end their own life, as it belongs to them. They are too afraid to give it a second thought. They think that even if they cannot solve their problem, at least they would not be alive to face it. From the causes of suicide we learn how intensively we need love, self-acceptance, meaning, purpose, hope, status, pride and forgiveness.

If suicide is the only solution to all the problems in the world, then nobody would be alive in this planet today. There is always hope, always a reason for a better life. Take a deep breath to understand this and then figure out how to solve the problem. Each new day can be a new beginning to forget the past and focus on the future. The rascals, ridiculous and the cowards commit suicide. One should always remember that life is meant to be lived. We must celebrate the one-time wonderful opportunity called life. We all have to die someday, but let that happen when it is designed and destined to happen. Let's not mess up with God's plan and give him a surprise in return. Let death be the way it is meant to be and not a 'self-service.'

Suicide is man's way of telling the God you can't fire me, ***I quit!***

- Bill Maher

Stage 8
Munna Bhai MBBS

Death is the cure for all diseases!

- Thomas Browne

"We are sorry, we tried our level best, but ultimately everything is in God's hand and we are not gods." This standard statement of many doctors after a patient's death is well-known. Medicine defines death as a stage in which the cessation of all the vital functions of the body occurs; the functions include heartbeat, respiration, brain activity, nervous system, blood circulation, kidney functions, digestive system, urinary duct and immune system. It's really very amazing that we all are born with more than 270 bones and die only with 206 bones!

Death is natural and normal. When the whole body or a part of the body that plays a vital role in the survival of the body, such as brain, heart, lungs, kidney, stomach, intestine, liver, pancreas, spinal cord and reproductive system, fails and if we don't find a replacement at the right time, death occurs. Nothing is dreadfully strange about this. There are no hidden mysteries about the process of dying in medical science. In the modern world, medicine has an answer for almost all the questions and doubts we could possibly have about the human body, its functions, types of diseases, medication, vaccination, curable and non-curable diseases.

It also explains what happens when, why and how? Death is irreversible. Once dead, always dead!

Today a person has a variety of diseases to choose from. The options are literally limitless. The most famous, hot and happening diseases of all times are heart attack, AIDS, kidney failure, brain tumour, brain death, nervous breakdown, stroke, paralysis, polio, food poisoning, high BP, low BP, dehydration, malaria, H1N1 and malnutrition. Of course, there are so many types of cancer, which literally consume any part of the body and spread everywhere like a wildfire. There is no curable medicine for cancer yet. Then there is diabetes, sugar, salt, spicy, what else? If not this, then that!

Once upon a time, the mortality rate of women during childbirth was very high. In hospitals, doctors were routinely examining corpses in the mortuary and then attending to women in childbirth, without washing their hands. This resulted in the death of the half the women who gave birth. The doctors themselves were spreading germs and bacteria from other patients. Doctors in those days believed that it was very common for women to die during child birth, as they saw many women dying. Many other people in the hospital too died because washing hands wasn't a routine procedure in the hospitals back then.

In the year 1847, an obstetrician (a doctor who deals in childbirth and delivery) named Ignaz Semmelweis proposed a theory: if the doctors wash their hands before examining and treating other patients, the mortality rates would greatly reduce. Semmelweis could not explain how washing hands was so effective in saving lives. He didn't know about germs, bacteria and virus and how they spread.

He observed that when a doctor washed his hands, the patients no longer caught fever, infection and any other diseases. He started doing this regularly, saving many patients' lives. When he told the other doctors this, nobody believed him. When he kept insisting on this over and over again, he was beaten up by guards. He died two weeks later from the injuries he suffered from the beating! I guess, they would belt him with those same unwashed hands.

In the following years, with the discovery of germs, bacteria and virus, doctors began to wash their hands. They even wore gloves while operating on patients. Today's hospitals are very hygienic. This didn't come easy. It came only after the loss of precious lives. Now with advancements in medical technology, there are several drugs, surgeries and treatments with which doctors can completely cure the patients in most cases. New types of diseases and cancers keep adding to the list each year. There are many patients in the world who are alive today only because of the 3Ms: medicine, machines and miracles.

Doctors and nurses deal with death every day. They give more than their best to save a patient's life, but they too have certain limitations. At the end of the day, even the doctors are just human beings. They can try to fix what they can. They can postpone the inevitable. But they cannot stop death altogether. Doctors can save a patient until the soul is present in the body. Once the soul is lost, life is lost. Even the best doctors from the world's best hospitals cannot bring back the dead. Doctors can save patients' lives or postpone their deaths; but in the end, can they save themselves from dying? If doctors cannot prevent themselves from dying, then how can we expect them to prevent and stop other patients from dying?

There are many diseases on the planet from which there is no recovery. At times, doctors give the maximum time left for the patient to live. This could be three months, six months, a year and so on. If the victim manages to outlive his time limit and shows signs of recovery, it is considered a medical miracle. And there are patients who die much before their given time.

Once a patient who was suffering from blood cancer was given six months to live. But when he failed to pay the hospital bills within those six months, he was given an additional six months to live, making sure he paid the bills by then. Cases have been registered where the patients have requested the doctors to take their lives as they didn't want to undergo so much pain and suffering (mercy killing).

In the present world, even after the death of a person, doctors, with the help of an autopsy, can tell how, why and when the patient died. There are several successful surgeries in which the patient's recovery and life is not guaranteed. Before the surgery, the patients' close relatives have to sign a disclosure agreement in which they say they are ready to face the consequences of the surgery and that they wouldn't blame the doctor or the hospital in the event of a mishap. This is not done for all surgeries, but only for those that have a slim chance of survival. The doctors proceed with the surgery with a general disclaimer, "We'll try our level best; the rest is in God's hands."

The human body is a fine piece of engineering complexity. The human body at times feels very strong and at times is very sensitive. Today, doctors are capable of transplanting not only eyes, skin, kidneys and liver, but heart and lungs too. These parts, including the blood, cannot be created in laboratories, we can only transplant them. There are millions of blind people residing on the planet right now and their numbers are increasing every day. We all are very lucky. Donate your eyes. Don't worry, the doctors are not going to take your eyes when you are alive. They won't make you blind to make others see. The eyes are taken only after your death. What will you do with your eyes after death? Let your eyes see the world even after you are gone.

Till date, no amount of development in science and medical technology has discovered proven methods to stop death. The physician cures, but it is nature that heals. Every birth says that God still loves us and every death states that He is still in control.

Stage 9
The Indian Philosophy

Death is not extinguishing the light.
It is only putting out the lamp because the dawn has come.
- Rabindranath Tagore

India is home to 1.2 billion people and counting. It is the world's second largest population and seventh largest country in terms of size. India is a land of rich traditions, cultural values and religious diversity. We have more than 3,000 castes and the highest number of languages spoken in a single country (fifty-seven). Our dance, music, food, clothing, art and architecture are diverse. India is the birth place of four religions: Hinduism, Buddhism, Jainism and Sikhism. India is a developing country and we have made a mark globally. We are no more just a land of snake charmers and elephants. India is also famous for its ancient teachings, philosophy, literature, yoga, meditation, Ayurveda, Vedic principles and countless other things.

According to the ancient Indian teachings, the human being is the ultimate form of all material forms of life. Humans are the greatest living entities on the planet. We have consciousness, higher reasoning power, logical thinking, a complex evolved brain, intelligence, adaptation, decision-making ability, and judgment skills. God made the human being the centre of all his creations. He made us in his own form. He gave us the power and authority over all of his other creations. God loves us!

The four basic activities of eating, sleeping, mating and defending are common to both human beings and animals. We human beings call ourselves 'civilised' because we eat fresh, healthy and cooked food on a clean plate on a dining table. We sleep on a soft mattress, rest our head over a mellow pillow and cover ourselves with a thick warm blanket in an air-conditioned room. We have sex in a nice bedroom of a well-furnished apartment. We use state-of-the-art weapons to defend and safeguard ourselves from our enemies.

But what the ancient Indian teachings preach is this: just because we eat, sleep, have sex and defend ourselves in a sophisticated way in a better place, it doesn't make us significantly more civilised than the animals. The activities still remain the same, there is no difference at all. The only difference is this: animals do their activities on the streets and we do them in the confines of our nice apartment. This cannot be defined as advancement and progress or make us any more civilised, just because we are better at doing things than the animals!

We human beings claim to be very sophisticated. With all the cutting-edge technology, scientific evolution, medical experiments, communication, computers, internet and mobile phones, our life was supposed to be exceptionally simpler, happier and easier than the lives of animals. But is it so? In order to fulfil our four basic needs, we have to work like a donkey. We are hardly happy with our lives. Sometimes we feel that animals have a better life than us. They too have to do the four basic things like us. People tend to believe that advancement of civilisation means improved ways of eating, sleeping, mating and defending, but these activities have nothing to do with civilisation. The fifth activity that human beings have to do and animals don't have to do is earn money.

The only thing that distinguishes us from the animals is we have consciousness and we can go in search of God. An animal cannot do this. We must use our consciousness to find God. The sole purpose of our life should be dedicated in the search of God. An animal cannot be forced to feel the presence of God and cannot be forced to worship Him. If a human being is not devoting himself towards God, then he is simply wasting his life. He is living the life of an animal.

Life is not possible without the presence of the 'soul.' The soul is the basic foundation of life. If the soul is removed from the body, the eyes cannot see, the mouth cannot speak and the ears cannot hear. The body is not alive anymore; it will be declared a dead body. The whole body is still in one piece, but it won't be animated anymore, because the soul is no longer present in the body.

The soul is infinitesimally microscopic, approximately the size of an atom. It is not visible to the naked eye, but that doesn't mean it doesn't exist. The soul is present in animals too, but unlike humans, animals don't have the consciousness to feel the soul.

The body that we have is just a material form. As long as the body is suitable to sustain life, the soul will be present in the body. Once the soul finds that the body is no longer usable, it leaves the body, transfers to another material body and a new life is born. Death is merely a process in which the soul gets transferred from one material body to another material body. Death is only for the body and not for the soul.

The sages believe that the body is not important. The body is just an instrument that carries the soul. The body is just the external physical appearance. We use it to perform our daily activities. There are approximately 8,400,000 material forms on earth. In this life, our soul resides in the human form, but once our body is no longer suitable for life, the soul leaves our body. So in our next life, our soul can be placed in any material body: ant, dog, cat, wild animal, insects, birds or maybe even human beings again. We don't know; we can't choose what we want to be in our next life. It is not under our control; it is God's will.

The sages believed that if we dedicate ourselves to the real purpose of our life, i.e. to find God and be aware of Him, then the soul will get enriched and enlightened. The person who finds God is the one who is not disturbed by anything material, has no desires, is free from all bodily urges and earthly temptations, treats himself as the spirit-soul and whose soul is dedicated to the quest of God and to honour Him and live life by His name. This person attains the highest perfection, enlightenment and salvation in life.

That is the reason why *sadhus* leave everything behind and go to the Himalayas to devote their lives to God. To achieve this highest form of perfection, they sacrifice all aspects of the material life such as money, fame, success, dreams, anger and sexual urge. Jesus, Buddha, Mahavira, Swami Vivekananda and Paramhansa Yogananda and others were not disturbed by anything material. The legitimate purpose of their lives was to find God and that's what they did. They dedicated their lives to discover God, to learn more and more about God and make people aware of Him.

We may notice that these days with the advancement in science and medicine, human survival has progressed a lot. The human body can survive without eyes, ears, hands and legs or just with one kidney or with the help of dialysis. The heart is very essential as it pumps blood throughout the body; the body cannot perform without it. The heart is the only organ in the body that never takes rest. But today we have found a replacement for the heart too. Artificial hearts (pacemakers) are costly, complex and fragile, but they still do the job. But no matter what kind of an expert the doctor is, how reputed the hospital is and how lucky the patient is (the doctor can even replace the heart and can save the patient), if the soul leaves the body, no doctor can bring the patient back from the dead. The patient is then declared dead. Where there is soul, there is life.

Stage 10
How Does Death Feel?

Don't send me flowers when I'm dead! I won't be able to accept them. If you like me, then send them when I'm alive.

- Brian Clough

In unfussy words, death can be defined simply as the absence of life. To simplify it further, it's just like: **"Birth – Something in between – Death!"** Our appointments are timely scheduled and death pays a visit to each one of us. So how is it to feel death? We may not be able to feel it with our senses as none of our sense organs will be functioning to endorse the sensations. But we can wonder about the amazing shadow death will cast on us.

Death is a bizarre condition in which we cannot think, talk, sense, touch, believe, pursue and do a thing. We are blind to look around us. All that exists is a thick black blanket of overwhelming darkness. We cannot even sense light. We don't hear a whispering chant. It is cautiously quiet, mind-bogglingly peaceful and there is a spell of profound silence. Despite the thunderous noise the world bombards us with, we cannot hear any gossip. Our nose is numb to sniff the disgusting 'fragrance' of our own body. There are no more growing nails and hairs to cut, nor growth in any part of the body. Forget our sixth sense, our five primary sensory organs fail to send the necessary information to the brain. As per studies, our sense of hearing is the last to go. Which means, we'd be still listening to what other people are speaking around us even after we're dead. But only for a very limited time! Within three days of death, the enzymes that once digested our dinner begin to eat us!

Summer, rain, winter, autumn and spring are the same. We neither require an umbrella on a rainy day nor a fur coat in the chilling winters. Every day is a Sunday. Yeah, why not? Regardless of which day it is for the rest of the world, every single day is a Sunday for the dead. A holiday. If you want every day to be a Friday, a Saturday or any other day, that is also not a problem. It will be done. You are the boss now. How creative can you be? We are on a long vacation, with boundless space and time, at a point of no return.

Death is an uninterrupted ever-lasting sleep. The only difference is we are not, by any means, waking up again. There won't be puzzling dreams or horrifying nightmares and definitely no sleep-walking. Nobody is at our side to listen to us, talk to us, take care of us, trust us and love us. We are obliged to withstand everything independently. No one is available to stretch a helping hand. If the living are 'online,' then the dead are 'offline.'

We can't go shopping, not even online shopping. We cannot avail ourselves of the home delivery service. We cannot download the trending apps, regret our mistakes, text or create a group on WhatsApp, update our status message, change our profile photo, like, comment and share or read the news feed on Facebook. Computers, mobile phones, internet, websites, social media and apps are only valid till we are thriving with life and blood.

In case you are planning to take your cellphone and laptop along with you when you are dead, there are no charging stations and free Wi-Fi zones out there. You may be a king, but do you know your crowning fate?

Death is like relaxing in a luxurious resort, round-the-clock. Each one of us gets to occupy a comfortable six-by-three feet executive suite. Mother earth may encounter earthquakes, volcanic eruptions, lightning, heavy rain, thunderstorms, floods, famine, economic crises, hunger, lack of clean water to drink and fresh air to breathe, epidemics and so on. But we don't have to be concerned. We hardly gave a damn when we were alive. Now we are rotten meat. What can we do now? Abso-bloody-lutely nothing! The problems, tensions, worries, crying, pain and vain are only for the living; not for those resting in peace. Death is a no-problem zone.

The world doesn't owe us anything. It is not going to run out of business just because we are bereft of life. We can no longer can make fake promises to break, there are no more rules and regulations to be followed, no more guessing games to be played, no breaks and no free time. Death is a full-time job. It requires our 100 per cent commitment. Nothing less will do. We don't have to earn money or pay any taxes. We don't have to impress anybody, be good to stupid people or be forced to do the things that we don't like. Forget respecting anybody, working our ass off and taking care of our health. All our fear, shyness, anger, stage fear, temper and fluctuating hopes are gone. Not a single soul is powerfully capable to disturb us and wake us up. We won't break people's trusts, hearts or bones. We will neither be judged nor be punished. There is total freedom and no injustice.

Death is a world with no place for love, feelings, emotions, sentiments, happiness, lust, ladies, sacrifices, education, birthdays, celebrations or vacations. There are no candle-light dinners. No more surprises, baby! We can be lazy once we die. We are not even expected to breathe. The heart does not require beating.

The heart starts beating while we are in our mother's womb. The heart knows no free time, sleep, laziness, Sundays or national holidays. It is the only organ that never takes rest. It beats continuously, is always alive with us and halts only when we are dead. It may slow down here and there or speed up while falling in love but it never stops (I wonder why it is called 'falling in love' and not 'rising in love.')

All the possessions we once owned are no longer ours. We are neither eligible to make peace with our past nor can we plan for our future. There is no career, pension, retirement and a future life. There is no luxury in knowing where we are, what we are doing, what time it is, what date it is and what day it is. We can't even get up, go out to on a brisk walk, feel the fresh air, savour the sheer beauty of the moon and the stars and sense the warmth of the sunlight. We cannot relax and we are extremely bored with no sort of entertainment. We can no longer start everything from the beginning. There are no more guests, visitors, messages, mails, spams, calls, stalkers, advertisements and newsletters. Anyway, who wants to meet the dead? How is it going to benefit anyone?

Maybe it is in death where loneliness is felt the most. The best part is we don't even realise that we are all by ourselves; that is the beauty of death. All we have to do is sleep for several thousand years. No amount of talking, shouting, crying, screaming, light, bad dreams, irritation, uneasiness, itching, temperature, thirst, piss, mosquito bite and alarm will wake us up. There are no worries of tomorrow as there isn't going to be any.

So get up and get to work when you have the time, energy, opportunity and life. We have a hell lot of time to be lazy, take rest, relax and sleep once we are dead. What else are we expected to do? What else can we possibly do? Go get a life!

Stage 11
Mummies ki Jaan!

Life and death are one thread,
the same line viewed from different sides.

- Lao Tzu

A mummy (not mother) is a dead body of either a human being or an animal whose skin and organs are preserved using chemicals, extreme cold, very low humid conditions and lack of air. The basic intention of mummifying a body is to place it in a cool and dry condition, wrapped with chemicals, to prevent the body from decaying further.

The process of mummification begins with the dehydration of the body. Water is the main ingredient that allows the body to decay once there is no life in the body. The procedure includes removing all the internal organs except the heart. The ancient Egyptians believed that the heart is the source of all feelings, emotions and thoughts that arise in a person. The dead still need the heart to pursue afterlife. The dehydration process alone takes twenty to thirty days on an average. Once the body is completely dehydrated, the mummy is wrapped in many layers of linen. The priests then place small amulets to guard the deceased from the evil. The body is then coated in resin to keep moisture away. The resin is also applied to the tomb. The mummy is then placed inside along with all the earthly goods the person once used. The tomb is sealed. In those days, people believed that the earthly things would help the dead in their afterlife.

The oldest mummy dates back to 5050 BC and it belongs to a child. The oldest known naturally mummified thing is a human head that goes back 8,000 years; it was found in the year 1936. When we hear the word mummy, the only thing that flashes in our minds is Egypt. But mummies of human beings and other animals have been found in several countries and continents such as Africa, Asia, Libya, Iran, Siberia, Philippines, Europe, Canary Islands, Czech Republic, Denmark, Hungary, Italy, North America, Canada, Greenland, Mexico, United States, Australia, New Zealand and South America. Over a million animal mummies have been found in Egypt alone, many of which are that of cats!

The ancient Egyptians had a beautiful belief about death and life thereafter. They believed that if dead bodies were not properly preserved, then the dead would lose the chance to experience afterlife. When their souls get to the entrance of heaven, the gods ask them two questions. Their answers determined whether they were admitted inside or not.

- Have you found joy in your life?
- Has your life brought joy to others?

Stage 12
The Ghost Protocol

Men die in despair and the ghosts die in ecstasy.

- *Honore Balzac*

How can a book on death be complete without talking about ghosts? *Hajmola ke bina, khaana kaise complete?* (how is a meal complete without Hajmola) There are several kinds of people on this planet and their beliefs, opinions, theories and traditions vary from each other. There are people who believe that ghosts exist but they haven't seen them. Some have heard about ghosts and others have felt their presence. Another set of people claim they have seen ghosts and have caught their activities red-handed.

There are folks who argue that there is no such thing as ghosts and that these beliefs are made up by human beings. They say it is all in their minds, thoughts and imagination, and in stories and movies, but not in the real world. Another group of people live in a dilemma; they are not sure whether ghosts exist or not. They are also not curious to discover the truth, but they are just scared to death to walk alone and talk about ghosts at night. They fear if they are alone, ghosts may attack them. This is what is in the back of their subconscious mind. Horror movies are perhaps responsible for their fear of ghosts.

The basic belief behind ghosts is this: ghosts are souls with unfulfilled desires. They didn't get a visa to heaven or hell, even if they did have the passport of 'death.' If a person dies with an unfulfilled desire or wish, he or she is forced to return to earth as free spirits. He or she comes back from being dead to fulfill the unfulfilled desire or wish.

I have heard about ghosts in stories, I have seen them in movies. From what I have read or seen, ghosts fall under two primary categories: the visible ghosts and the invisible ghosts. The visible ghosts are seen by the naked human eye and the invisible ones are, well, invisible. Some ghosts are believed to have supernatural powers. They attract attention with their powers. They seem as though they can do almost anything.

Ghosts can be further classified into three categories: the good ghosts, the bad ghosts and the revenge ghosts.

The ghosts that rise back from the dead to do something good, maybe for their family members, relatives, friends or lovers, without scaring or harming anybody are the good ghosts. They come to the earth, serve their purpose of visit and go back quietly. These ghosts are rare.

The ghosts that come back from the dead, scare people and harm them are referred to as bad ghosts. These ghosts don't have a specific target. They attack strangers and loners at night and scare them to death. They don't have any particular intention. They may be deeply hurt by the way others had treated them when they were alive. But the people who harmed, tortured, punished or killed them are also dead. So they find satisfaction in causing harm to other people in society. They are doing all this for time-pass, for entertainment. What else do they've to do? There are recorded incidents where ghosts entered other people's bodies and forced them to hurt and, at times, even kill themselves. Human beings have devised tactics to deal with such ghosts by talking to them and convincing them to leave the bodies they have occupied.

The revenge ghosts are the ones who come back from the dead with a specific purpose. They may have been murdered by someone or their families may have been troubled by someone. These ghosts seek revenge. They have a distinct set of enemies and they are back only to harm or kill them. They do not pay attention to others, they do not harm others. Once their mission is accomplished, they go back to where they came from.

Some ghosts choose to reside in a big bungalow and operate from there. This is why the movies call it a 'haunted house'. The ghosts from the grave come here for campus placements and attend the interview. They are then placed according to the necessity and requirement. There are beliefs that if a person commits suicide, his soul roams around in the house. There are crazy people in this world who go in search of these haunted houses to understand and hunt down ghosts and communicate with them. There are also people who go in search of ghosts, using techniques such as the Ouija board.

Ghosts are not accepted by society. They do not have the freedom to wander in public among living people. Well, we do not know for sure whether they exist or not. There are many references to them in history. A few ghosts have also been captured and recorded on cameras. The horror movies are the main reason for people's perception of ghosts and the fear towards them. How far is the concept of ghosts true? No one knows. Ghosts do not reveal their trade secrets, do they?

Stage 13
Who Will Cry When We Die?

The dead cannot cry out for justice.
It is a duty of the living to do so for them.

- Lois Bujold

The water flowing has suddenly stopped. The fish is out of the sea. The tree has shed all its leaves. The flying bird has lost its wings. The raging fire has now calmed down. The brightly glowing candle has been put out. The vehicle has run out of fuel. The body is still there in one piece, but it is not animated anymore, because the soul is no longer present in the body. This results in a lifeless body. A dead body.

Well, we may be poor, rich, a student, young, famous, successful, politician, a proud father, the mother of three children or old. Who is going to be present on our big day at our funeral? Who will bid us goodbye on the final day of our earthly life? Who is going to see us for one last time, wave us a final goodbye and shed a few tears on our grave?

I have always wanted to attend my own funeral. I want to watch from a corner all the people who made it to my funeral. Who are those people who are honestly mourning for me? I would like to know how many are acting and pretending to cry. How many are possibly happy? I want to watch them, at least in the form of a housefly if not a human being. If this wish of mine is granted, then I will be one step ready to die.

How fascinating would it be in reality if we get a chance to attend our own funeral? We would be able to see all the people with whom we had spent our entire life. The people whom we cared for, trusted, loved, believed in and lived our lives for. Perhaps many of them wouldn't even make it to our funeral. They may have better things to worry about in their own lives rather than attend a funeral. Who attends our funerals and what their reactions are based on how we lead our lives. How much good have we done to them? It's not who they are, it's what you mean to them that counts.

So, how many people do you think would attend your funeral – 5, 10, 25, 50, 100, 250, 500, 1000 or more? Who are these people? Are they your family, grandchildren, relatives, distant relatives, friends, Facebook friends, Twitter followers, ex-girlfriends, ex-spouses, well-wishers, fans, enemies, drivers, watchmen, neighbours, business partners, office colleagues, old age home friends, local people, native people, passers-by or strangers? Who are the strangers and passers-by? Who even bothered to invite them? Why do they attend your funeral? You will never know. Well, does it matter who they are?

The people at our funeral shed a few tears, say a few prayers, place flowers on our grave, and wish us a happy journey to heaven. After that the drama is over. The curtains close and we are buried deep down in the earth or body is burnt, depending on which religion we belong to. But this doesn't make any difference. We won't be able to come back from the dead even if we can or if we want to.

I have attended many funerals. I have observed people closely. If the person who has died is young (for instance, a student, not married, just married or has small children), then there is a possibility of more people crying. People feel sad that the deceased was so young. They wonder who would take care of his or her children or what would happen to his or her parents.

But if one dies after fifty or sixty, people may say he or she was at the fag end anyway. If a person dies after a long illness or was hospitalised for a long time, a handful of people will cry. They may be the deceased person's children, grandchildren, spouse or very close relatives. If someone dies of an illness at an old age, people tend to say, "He was sick for a long time. His time was up. He has suffered a lot in hospitals. Instead of suffering, it's better to die… At least he had a good death." Some even go a step further and say, "It was a miracle that he made it for so many days."

Once we are buried, people have better things to worry about. They recover quickly, sooner than you expect them to. They come back to their senses and even start using their sense of humour. I have seen it a number of times. Nobody gives a shit, man! People don't value the dead. The dead are a 'closed chapter' that nobody wants to reopen.

Some people cry for a few days or a few weeks. Some people are practical and move on with their lives immediately. I don't know who is right. But it doesn't matter who is right. The dead are not going to come back alive whether we cry or are happy. But I feel it is our basic duty to mourn for the dead. We are also going to die someday. But how would we feel if people laugh, party and celebrate our death?

It is true that the dead are not capable of knowing. Still… Who knows? We may get to watch our funeral from above. Live 4 K telecast at heaven or hell may be possible. Do we want to see people laughing at our funeral? It's him today, tomorrow it's you and me.

Oh dead man! Where is all the money that you earned all your life? You did a whole lot of things to earn that money, didn't you? You didn't give your family enough time. You worked so hard all the time to earn all that money. Whose money is that going to be now? Will your money, assets and property documents be placed in your coffin so that you lead a luxurious life in heaven? If heaven exists, then it will not be like earth. Heaven will treat everyone the same way, regardless of how much money we had on earth.

A wise old man once said, "When man is eighteen years of age, he thinks that the whole world is busy thinking about him all the time. When he is forty years of age, he doesn't give a damn about what other people think about him because he has a family and children to take care of. When he is sixty years of age, he realises that nobody was ever even bothered about him."

Unfortunately, people SURPRISE us! They don't give a damn about what we think, say or do. At the end of the day, everybody has their own life to take care of. They will be busy doing what they want and going where they want to go. But there are a few people who genuinely care for us; they are certainly worried about us. Our thoughts and actions affect them, they believe in us and rely on us. They are very hard to find. The sad thing is there are very few of them. Identify them, because they are the ones who really matter. They help you lead a life filled with happiness and peace of mind; they make life meaningful and worth living for. Once you are dead, they are the ones who will cry for you, carry you to the graveyard and bury you. Don't lose them when you are alive. Make sure you know who will cry when you die.

Stage 14
Life in Easy Installments

Life is too short to worry about anything.
You better enjoy it, because the next day promises nothing.

- Eric Davis

Mankind is gifted with a lifespan of 100 years and yet there is nothing called as 'the right age to die.' Yes, there are a handful of fortunate people who have made it for more than 100 years, but we are speaking about the standard lifetime here. The average life expectancy in India today is roughly sixty-five to seventy years. The oldest person to live on the surface of the earth is Jeanne Calment of France, who died in 1997 at the age of 122 years and 164 days. The oldest person still living in the planet is Jeralean Talley, aged 117 years.

A century is a benchmark. But is it certified that everybody, beyond any shadow of doubt, lives for a brimming 100 years? How many of us can say with confidence that we will celebrate our 100th birthday when we know can die from anything, anytime and anywhere?

Let us assume that by hook or by crook we flourish for 100 years. How much time do we have in hand? Have we genuinely experienced our life to the fullest extent or are we barely surviving? Let us do a calculation of the years that we live to months and break it down further.

1 year =12 months

100 years = 1,200 months

Now, let us evaluate the number of days we get to live on earth. Remember, all calculations are made using the standard lifespan for human beings.

1 year = 365 days

100 years × 365 days = 36,500 days

+ 25 days of leap years

36,500 + 25 = **36,525 days**

Is that it? An individual can live a maximum of 36,525 days in his 100 years from cradle to grave. We expected more, right? This seems way too less. But for how many years people authentically spin off to live? Now let's determine the number of hours, minutes and seconds that we comprehend to breathe.

1 day = 24 hours

Number of days in 1 lifetime = 36,525 days

36,525 days × 24 hours = 876,600 hours

876,600 hours = 52,596,000 minutes

52,596,000 minutes = 3,155,760,000 seconds

So every single second, each minute and hour, every passing day, week, month and year is counting. The time just flies. For no reason does it take a break. We waste our time, eat, drink, exercise, sleep, watch TV, travel, work, take a break, go on vacations, wait for the bus, and wait for the right moment to start any task. The clock keeps ticking. Human beings haven't invented time travel or the ability to pause time yet. The mechanical clock's battery can run out of charge or our watch may stop working, but life's clock runs uninterrupted. Time, tide, and 'power cuts' wait for none.

In our lives, we have certain fundamental things that every human being and animal has to do. The foundations of human survival are eating and sleeping. We cannot disregard these two vital things regardless of who and where we are. In order to live a healthy, strong and sound life, for the proper growth of our body and to keep the brain in a perfectly good condition, we need to sleep for seven to eight hours every day. This implies not only to humans, but also to animals, birds and insects. Now, let us enumerate how much time we spend in a life cycle snoozing. Let's grant eight hours to sleep in a period of twenty-four hours. We allocate one-third of our daily life to sleep. There are some people who catnap just for four to six hours on weekdays, but sleep for twelve to fourteen in the weekends. So ultimately, everyone more or less sleeps for the same number of hours across a week. (The recommended sleep hours for an adult are seven to eight hours, nothing less will do.)

1 day = 24 hours

1 day – 8 hours of sleep

1 week – 56 hours of sleep

1 month – 240 hours of sleep

1 year – 2,920 hours of sleep

Hours in a year = 365 days × 24 hours = 8,760 hours

So in one year we sleep for around 2,920 hours or roughly 3,000 hours out of 8,760 hours in a year. This is again the standard snoozing duration. We all have a habit to suspend our consciousness for long hours, quite often. Sleeping feels so peaceful, soothing and comforting. Every morning we are in a *fevi*-bonded relationship with our beds.

Now, let us calculate how many years we spend in our life cycle just sleeping and dreaming.

1 year = 2,920 hours of sleep

2,920 hours × 100 years = 292,000 hours

292,000 hours = 12,166 days

12,166 days = 405 months

405 months = **33 years**

Roughly we spend 30–35 years in our life sleeping.

What? Wonderful, isn't it? Then why don't we reward ourselves a mushy comfortable mattress? Never compromise on your bed and boots, because you spend most of the time in your lifespan in them. Do give this a thought.

Well, now we have computed only the time taken to sleep in our lifetime. However, there are other activities we undertake for our survival. Every day we need to have coffee, breakfast, lunch, dinner, snacks and so on. Besides chewing gum, partying and dreaming, there are other mandatory things that have to be accomplished, such as brushing, bathing, answering nature's calls and loo breaks. Let us assume these activities consume 2.5 hours in a day.

1 day – 2.5 hours

1 year – 912.5 hours

100 years – 91,200 hours

91,200 hours = 3,800 days

3,800 days = 126 months

126 months = **10.55 years**

In the course of 100 years, we spend thirty to thirty-five years only to sleep and ten to twelve years just to eat and do other mandatory activities. According to research, an average human being spends three years of his lifetime in the washroom. A survey found: Men spend almost a year of their lives just staring at women! Let us round this to forty-five years.

KABOOM! How many years remain for us to live?

Do we even have enough time?

Of the remaining fifty-five years, five to six years are spent in premature childhood, which we hardly remember. We don't remember what happened, all we recall is we were happy then. Thereafter, we go to school for a real long time period, then comes college and higher studies and maybe even correspondence courses. We spend hours and hours with our boyfriend/girlfriend, in addition talking over the phone and texting. We go on dates, we spend several hours on Facebook, browse the internet for time-pass and play video games and mobile games.

As soon as we graduate, we start looking for a job. Some find a job soon, some take two to three years to find the right job. Once in the job, we work for eight to twelve hours a day, five to six days a week. Employment devours a major chunk of our lives. Then we get married and raise a family. We spend time with our family and friends. On top of everything, we are lazy. Sometimes we don't understand how to kill time. Moreover, there are Sundays and holidays, in which we seldom do anything worthwhile.

If life is a vehicle, then the days in it are the fuel. Each person can have a maximum of 36,525 litres (days) of fuel. Unfortunately, there is no refueling. Life is just one tank full of fuel. Once the tank is empty, life is over. You are done, it's gone. It is up to each one us to decide where to go and what to do with the fuel of life. You are the owner of the vehicle of life. Your parents, relatives, friends, wife and children maybe the pillion riders, but you have to drive the vehicle. No one else can do it for you.

A few months pass this way…maybe a few more years aimlessly and then we find ourselves in old age, where there is a wide variety of diseases to choose from, including the sweet disease diabetes. Back pain and poor memory are mandatory to every old person. Several people have deadly diseases such as heart problems and cancer. In old age, there isn't anything much we can do, as we won't have the same energy we had earlier. We can't just run, dance and jump around like before. Most of old age is spent sleeping, watching TV, sitting in the park, walking, talking, and in the worst case, we may be spending time at an old age home or a hospital. And then we kick the bucket 'one fine day,' leaving everything behind.

So when do we have the time to live? What else do we do in our lifetime? We party, watch TV, watch movies and travel. Speaking about watching TV, many Indian women are TV serial addicts. Many watch five to ten serials in a single day. TV serials run for years and years; they feel like forever. People spend at least two to three hours a day watching serials, sports, movies, reality shows and news. Now calculate how many years they squander just watching TV? Oh my god! Watching TV is a huge waste of time. Nothing else will even come close to it in being a time waster.

I live in *namma* Bengaluru. The city is notorious for a lot of things, but it is most remembered for its terrible traffic jam. I once travelled two hours to reach office and another two hours to get back home. Many of my friends are still doing the same. For eight hours of office work, we agonise for four hours on the road. This eats up a lot of time in a day and in our lifetime too.

From all these calculations, we realise that we have very limited time for ourselves. Life is awfully short to be wasting time each passing day. Occasionally, we spend oodles of hours doing nothing. We just loiter around, unaware of how badly it is going to cost us in the final run. Every single second and minute, once played out, will not be given back to us. Don't we often wonder these? *Oh, it's already another year? I remember celebrating New Year just a few days ago. How did an entire year race by so quickly?*

In the bat of an eyelid, years and years pass by. One year, two years, five years, ten years and a lifetime…

People say time is money. No. Time is life. Because time is what life is made up of. Time wasted is life wasted. How long has your life promised to stay with you? Death maybe tomorrow's guest. Do we know that? Are we prepared? Have we lived our life ethically? Did we discover the true purpose of our life? We are here for a defined period of time. We may never get this chance ever again. So there is unmistakably no point in wasting our valuable time on earth. Life is exceptionally small. Make the most of it when you own one. Wasted money can be earned again. But we cannot get back wasted time. Time is more valuable than money. We can get more money, but we cannot get more time! So stop wasting time thinking about the wasted time! One day we will become aware of all the mistakes we made and want to make up for them, but we cannot make up for lost time.

STAGE 15

THE ADVANTAGES OF DEATH

Death does not concern us, because as long as we exist, death is not here. And when it does come, we no longer exist.

- Epicurus

For people, death is a lifetime enemy. They hate it all their lives. They find it complicated and disastrous and try to escape it. But death offers certain advantages.

Once dead, we don't need money, we don't even have to earn money. We don't need to breathe, eat and drink, because we are never going to be thirsty or hungry. We don't even have to wake up early in the morning. We won't find ourselves complaining about lack of sleep, as we would be lying deep down in the earth all the time once we are dead.

There is no more respiration, digestion, emotion, observation, meditation, education, relation, ambition, religion, dedication, concentration, assumption, anticipation, expectation, exception, presentation, promotion, profession, recession, option, opinion, rejection, demotion, domination, addiction, sensation, seduction, satisfaction, celebration, vacation, tension, irritation, erection, ejaculation, infection, frustration, depression, masturbation, menstruation and loose motion.

There is no more studying, going to school, homework, getting a degree, projects, assignments, seminars, tests, exams, results, supplementary tests, higher studies, career, future, job, working hard, salary, meetings, sales, targets, deadlines, reports, video conferences, overtime, appraisal, being professional, missing the cab, bank balance, economic crisis, listening to our boss/manager/team leader, bending down, adjusting, getting fired, going to the gym, saving money, being consistent, punctual, open-minded and disciplined, following rules, regulations, terms and conditions, replying to e-mails, answering calls, giving missed calls or dialling the wrong numbers.

Death puts an end to the need for being patient and humble, being human, being proud of one's goals, purpose, power, prestige and status. There is no need to show courtesy, be sympathetic, kind, polite or help others. You don't have to try to forget the past. There are no more crushes, lust, love at first sight, commitments, relationships, sentiments, doubts, break-ups, loneliness, sadness, sorrows, worries, miseries, mysteries, revenge, anger, jealousy, selfishness, fear, shame, insults, embarrassments, awkward moments, honesty, anxiety, shock, stage fear, pressure, strain, stress, cholesterol, calories, vanity, punishment, torture, sins, free advice, rumours, gossips, boredom, tired or laziness.

Death puts a full stop to jogging, exercising, hurrying, dieting, working, thinking, planning, fixing, reading, doing, waiting, executing, meeting, dating, texting, hoping, promising, understanding, loving, missing, caring, sharing, sacrificing, compromising, trusting, marrying, kidding, regretting, misunderstanding, lying, cheating, hating, losing, paining, sobbing, feeling, crying, punishing, divorcing, let going, forgiving, thanking, winning, speeding, sneezing, cleaning, washing, cooking, shaving, itching, misusing, misfiring, vomiting, and shitting. Something, anything, everything, no more NOTHING!

And there is no more fear of cold, fever, cough, sugar, diabetes, back pain, cancer, sexually transmitted diseases, heart attacks, kidney failures, epidemic diseases, headaches, visiting the dentist/doctor, staying healthy, worrying about our growing tummy, weight gain, weight loss, or maintaining the figure. We don't have to pay insurance premium, penalties, fines, fees and taxes. There are no more terrorist attacks, natural calamities, war, nightmares, and income tax raids. We don't have to work from home, there are no losses, emergencies, disasters or breaking news. Brushing the teeth, taking a shower, being a failure, trying to quit smoking or drinking, saving money for the future, drinking and driving, having medicines and combatting diseases are all matters of the past.

We don't have to pay taxes, take bullshit from people, work our ass out, warm-up or listen to our spouses. And there are no more headaches from girlfriends (Okay, I am just kidding, babes.) We don't have to do yoga, say sorry, pay back our loans/debts, pay credit card bills, electricity bills, phone bills, internet bills, rent and EMIs. We don't have to bother looking good and stylish. We don't have to wait for the holidays because every day is a holiday. Once dead, we are on a permanent holiday. We don't have to worry about global warming or work for world peace. The best part is: nobody will even be BUSY anymore!

Not a single soul is going to order us, threaten, arrest, blame, scold, yell, get mad at us, give advice, guide, control, and dominate us. Nobody is going to kidnap or murder us. No more cases will be filed against us and nothing will be illegal. We don't owe anything to anybody anymore. We don't have to respect anyone, use bad and harsh words, take care of people, say goodbye, mess up things, wait or get caught. There are no more accidents, jet lags, turbulence, delays and lunch breaks. There are no more problems and no more solutions.

The lights have to turn off after sometime, someday. Then everything will become silent, dark, quiet, calm and peaceful. Nobody lives forever. There is no one to disturb us, no one steals anything from us. Well, what are we left with to steal? No summer is too hot, no wind blows too fast, no earthquake is too shaky and no winter is too cold. Everything comes to an end with death. The train has reached its final destination. Game over! The best part is we don't have to die again. Why? Yeah, you guessed it right. I knew it! You are a genius!

So even death has its advantages. Some advantages sound very good, but the only hitch is this: no matter what happens to the world, who cries out in pain, how much ever somebody needs us, remembers us and misses us, we cannot go back to being alive. There is no known possible way to break free and escape from the cage of death. Death isn't a *Prison Break or The Shawshank Redemption.* And we cannot be *Sherlock Holmes* to figure a way out.

The advantages death offers are worth waiting for, they are praiseworthy. Anyway, all these are mandatory advantages: they are for everyone who is dead. The one thing in common is: we don't have an option. Whether we like it or hate it, we must get used to it. We have to take it. Can we do something to alter our destiny? No. What can we do for time-pass? There is no entertainment after death.

No matter what happens to the world and how much worse it gets, we are always silent, calm, quiet, peace-loving, numb and simply dead. Death comes with its own set of advantages too; we just have to see it the other way around.

Stage 16
Is There Something We Can Do?

To himself everyone is immortal; he may know he is going to die, but he can never know that he is 'dead.'

- Samuel Butler

We wish we could defer death, but we cannot. No one can. Despite the ground-breaking advancements in science, technology and medicine, we cannot change death. Even in the distant future, whether we find life on the surface of Mars, whether or not aliens get in touch with us or no matter how efficacious we are in our biological experiments, neither God nor science can stop death.

When the Grim Reaper meets us, he doesn't give a damn whether we are happy, sad, angry, afraid, unconscious, retired, a virgin, sick, eating, starving, having a hot shower, dreaming in sound sleep, making love, driving, playing a sport, flying a plane, on an adventurous holiday, hospitalised or of a tender age. The reaper bears no soft corner or centre for anyone and doesn't care to listen to our explanations. He doesn't wait for us to be wide awake before taking us away. Once he appears in front of us, he is in no mood to appreciate our lame excuses. If truth be told, we have just one option: lie down, admit defeat and surrender ourselves, heart to soul, in his vast extended arms. We can only take it. Unfortunately, we cannot leave it.

Let's assume that our time is up, but it is a weekend. When death arrives at our door step, we are in no position to say, "Please allow me to savour my last weekend. I really don't want to die on a weekend. You come and pick me up on Monday." No babe, you cannot say that. Death is undeniable, predestined and full of authority. No sentimental feelings, punch dialogues and cascade tears are going to serve as a defence mechanism.

Several people love the thrill of an adventurous life. Adventure gives them the kick to live. Adventure in plain English means to risk life to death by a few inches. Many things fall under the adventure category: sky diving, trekking, bungee jumping, racing, rash driving, river rafting, hunting and so on. The success of an adventure is in returning home safely, alive in one piece. If we die during an adventure activity, then it won't be referred to as an adventure anymore. People may call it a risky or stupid venture. So adventure in other words means to risk your life and return home safely.

On November 27, 2014, Phil Hughes, a fabulous cricketer, just twenty-five years old, died from a bouncer. The bouncer has been used in cricket for more than 100 years now. How did he die? Just like that? Was it the way that the ball bounced? Was it his helmet that had a design flaw or was it his fate?

Paul Walker, a car enthusiast and the legendary actor from the *Fast and Furious* series and other movies, died in a car accident. The car he was in crashed into a concrete lamp-post and two trees. The car was travelling at the speed of 160 km an hour on November 30, 2013. Paul Walker had made a statement couple of years ago: one day if speed kills me, don't cry, because I was smiling. Did Paul Walker predict his own death and did he know how he would die?

Mahatma Gandhi, the father of our nation, was assassinated on January 30, 1948 by Nathuram Godse, just five months after India got its independence from the British rule. Did Gandhi know before this incident that he was going to be shot dead?

NO! Death can be very surprising at times. It is very good at giving surprises. It is the last surprise that we will ever see and undergo. Does anyone get to know in advance when they are going to die, so that we can be prepared and try not to act surprised when death arrives? We really don't get that chance until and unless we are in a critical stage after an accident, suffering from any deadly disease or we are really old and weak and realise that there is going to be an appointment with death soon. But it is tough to predict when exactly death will come knocking.

Death doesn't come with a price tag. It is free and mandatory. Death isn't a prize distribution ceremony after a game; it is "**The beginning of the end.**" So are you prepared? How is it all going to end? Who will be around you when you are taking your last big breath? Who is going to take care of you? Who will give you a glass of water or order a pizza if you feel like eating one, before you die? I hope the pizza delivery guy comes within thirty minutes, before the ambulance arrives. Because if he comes late, even if the pizza is free, you will no longer be alive to eat It! LOL! Don't worry, your pizza will definitely be delivered in thirty minutes.

In the midst of all the confusion about death, the one striking question is: is there something we can do about death? Can death ultimately forgive us, give us a hug and set us free to live forever? Does death have a good sense of humour or is it strict, disciplined and punctual? How much money can we give death as a bribe for forgiving us? Does death care for money? Why would death need money? What would it do with billions of dollars? Well, does death ask for anything else? Does death expect us to give anything? Can we ask death to give us life? Nothing more, nothing less, just life?

So is there something we can do to stop death? No! Nothing. All we can do is use our life for a respectable cause and make the best of it when we have one. Life is singular. This is it! This is all what we have got. This isn't a trial, a warm-up or a practice session. This is real. There are no second chances. It's like a one day cricket match with limited number of overs. We get to play all the overs provided we are not out. So watch your step; run-outs are like accidents. Make wise decisions. Make every shot count. Life is finite, not infinite.

Stage 17
She may not be a Babe; but She Sure Ain't a Bitch!

Life is hard. Then you die. Then they throw dirt in your face and finally the worms eat you. Be grateful it happens in that order.

- David Jerrold

As a matter of fact, everyone indubitably hates death. No one's dream is to die. Nevertheless, it supervenes us or to others. We may or may not mourn over the death of others, but most of us will at least show some anguish and horror. Attending others' funerals remind us of our own. It happens to me. I think about my death when I hear that someone has died or if I attend any funeral. I start imagining how my funeral would be.

Death results in losing a person permanently. He or she is not going to reappear ever again. Death plays by its own set of rules; we are not gifted to see the game-plan. We don't even have the authority to alter what is destined to us, until and unless it is suicide. All we can do is accept the way death is. Termination may possibly possess an atom, a nucleus, a proton or an electron. It may be positively or negatively charged. It doesn't matter. People still die from electric shocks.

Electricity is one of the most incredible inventions of mankind till date. It is ironic that water generates electricity, but once electricity is born, water becomes its predominant enemy. Electricity has evolved as a basic necessity along with money, mobile phone, Wi-Fi, food, water, shelter and clothing. Today's generation may manage to live even without food, water and oxygen, but not without mobile phone and Wi-Fi.

DEATH. Whoa! It is scary, creepy, interesting, complicated, mandatory, undeniable and miraculous. It brings too many questions and exclamations. Life was supposed to be fun, simple, easy and happy. Why has it become a headache for us? We have too many problems, attractions, distractions, addictions and temptations. What is the secret behind life? What was God thinking when He was creating us? Why did He create us? All our ancestors are dead and long gone. Where are they? In heaven? What are they doing now? Just sleeping and rotting or enjoying the bliss of heaven or being punished in hell? We don't know, we can only presume and presuppose. We wait to get old without realising that we can always be old but never young again. Living isn't just about surviving, is it?

We may perish anywhere, anytime and in any way, without any prior warning. Death is at all times lurking somewhere out there. It keeps an eye on us, like God. Sometimes in life, we all experience a fraction of a second when we believe it is our last moment on earth. Those 'missed situations' happen especially while driving, crossing the road, climbing up or down a staircase, or slipping on a wet surface. Remember, you could have died at those times. But fortunately, nothing happened. Brace yourself. You are still alive today reading this.We never know when we are going to die; that is the revolving mystery of life.

Death is not a guest. It is not the point where the hero meets the heroine in slow motion at the top of a mountain or at a waterfall. Death is definitely not a villain too. It is the way life is. That is how life has been planned, engineered, routed, designed and destined. Life is a one-way trip to death, the final destination. Every place along the road is just another pit-stop. There is no other preferable option to choose from. Death is everyone's cup of tea.

Death may not be the most beautiful twenty-four karat solid gold thing that happens to us, but her purity is guaranteed. She knows no politics, plays no double games and can certainly be trusted. She will without doubt approach every last one of us on earth, as promised. She is fool-proof, doesn't have a duel mind, isn't confused, doesn't lie and doesn't make any fake promises. There are no national holidays, entrance exams, interviews, previous experiences, minimal educational qualification; it's both for the literate and the illiterate.

We don't have to submit a passport-sized photograph or ID proof to death. She knows who we are. Our relatives may need to produce these proofs to get our death certificate, but we don't need to show any proof to death. Death has no demands, requirements, expectations, special instructions or conditions. Death is not greedy. She is neither a fantasy nor a miracle. There may be pain and suffering at the time of death, but once dead everything becomes neutral, calm and peaceful. She makes us "rest in peace" forever, till the end of time. There is no past, present or future. Death may not be a babe, but she sure isn't a bitch!

Stage 18
Living Forever!

Dying is easy, it's the living that scares me to death.

- Annie Lennox

Wow! A world without death sounds delicious, right? But how will the world be with this essence of reality? What if every soul is destined to dwell on earth till hell freezes over? What if not a single individual is going to die? Is it possible to even articulate this condition? People should and will die if we kill them, if they meet with a grievous accident, if they contract some deadly disease like AIDS and cancer or if they commit suicide, right?

But let's say people stay out of harm's way by evading accidents and avoiding fatal diseases, nobody kills them and they don't commit suicide, then they could theoretically live forever. We get older and, at the age of fifty, natural ageing stops. Thereafter, we won't be growing anymore. It becomes our responsibility to take care of our lives, provided there are no external threats.

In this new reality, all the stupendous people who changed the world, such as Socrates, Chanakya, Aristotle, Aryabhatta, Benjamin Franklin, Pablo Picasso, Albert Einstein, Bruce Lee, Neil Armstrong, Walt Disney and Mother Teresa would be alive today on planet earth. Well, if not all, at least some of them would definitely be alive.

Now these are the eminent people. What about the evil people who destroyed the earth and killed thousands of innocent people such as Adolf Hitler, Saddam Hussein and Osama Bin Laden? Then they too would be among us, right? That doesn't sound admissibly cool. In that case, the world would have been hardly vindicated to sustain life.

If there was no way to die naturally, the world would have been a dangerous place to live in. Everybody would have been busy fetching each other's lives or else everybody would live forever, right? The world would have been a place where only the fittest survived. Humanity would have turned into wolves maybe!

Coming back to reality, despite the fact that we can live a maximum of 100 years, these years are not guaranteed to everyone. People fizzle out at different ages and stages. In this awfully inadequate lifespan of ours, we have all the time to waste by doing things for mere entertainment and amusement. Sometimes we just don't understand how to spend time productively. We do jobs that we don't like. We sleep extra-long hours as it is extremely soothing. People watch TV to kill their time. There is absolutely nothing wrong in doing all these things. It's a matter of choice what an individual wants to do with his or her life. But think about this: if we are spending a lot of time doing nothing valuable in a short lifetime, imagine what would happen if there was no death at all. What would happen if we are destined to "live forever?" Imagine how lazy mankind would be! Nearly everyone would be eating, sleeping or watching TV for a record amount of the time.

Even in a short lifespan, people tend to dislike each other and are jealous of others' growth. They develop trust, only to break it. People are impatient, angry, vengeful and plot against their enemies. They stop talking and start cursing. Money is everything to them. They don't value relationships and do not think it is essential to be loving. People go after money, power, status, possessions, property and business. So what kind of a scenario would unfold if there was no death at all?

Death was also born at the time that life came into existence.The opposite of life is not unlife or dislife, it is death. Where there is life, there is, of course, death too. Death has been in existence for long, it still exists and it will continue to exist till the cessation of life itself. Life isn't genuinely worth living if everyone lives forever. There will be no tension, struggle and tears. All we have to do is make sure nobody kills us, there are no accidents and deadly diseases, and we don't commit suicide. But this doesn't sound right, does it? Death should exist. If there is a beginning, then there must be an end too. If life starts someday, then it has to stop someday. That is how life was designed and destined to be and that's how it is. No one can live till doomsday. But just in case, figuratively speaking, what if there was no death at all?

Stage 19
The Grand Finale!

I would rather die a meaningful death,
than live a meaningless life.

- Corazon Aquino

Now, let's say your time has arrived. Somehow you come to know that all you are left with is twenty-four hours, before you are taken away and there is no coming back. What do you want to do in the final twenty-four hours of your life? Where do you want to go? Who do you want to see and talk to? Who will you call?

Do you wish to forgive or apologise to someone? Do you want to tell someone that you love him or her? Do you want to regret your mistakes, tell the truth, write something down, eat something special, smoke a cigarette, have a drink, go on a date, make love, go to office, work, go to a party, sleep, recall fond memories, go on a long drive or do something adventurous such as trekking, skydiving, bungee jumping and scuba diving? Do you want to watch TV, go to a movie or listen to your favourite songs? Serial addicts out there, how many of you want to see the last episode of your favourite serial?

Do you want to go for a final round of shopping? Do you want to lavishly spend all the money you have earned in your lifetime? Do you want to search for your insurance papers, write a will, spend time with your family, children, grandchildren and friends or do something to kill time? Do you want to be alone or do you want more time to understand and digest the fact that you are going to die tonight? Do you want to start praying to God and ask him for bonus time or mercy? Do you want God to forgive all your sins and send you to heaven? Do you want to mourn your own death or do you want to go out and make some money before you finally leave this planet?

You can do whatever you want. It is going to be your cup of coffee; after all, it is your life! But the time left on your clock is only twenty-four hours. How often do you stare at the clock to see the time? Maybe today you will finally realise that time runs very fast, faster than you expected it to.

The life you have lived so far may flash before your eyes: your childhood, school days, college life, teenage, first love, first job, friends, mistakes, adulthood, marriage, children, family, retirement, old age and everything else. These images may play out in front of your eyes like a movie. You are the hero, of course! It is your movie and it is your life. Will you think about the good and bad you did to others? Do you really think you will be happy about the bad things you did in your life? Will you be happy that you had anger and revenge inside you all these years? What is the one thing you always wanted to do in your life, but never did? May be you were too afraid to do it or you never got the time, chance, courage, motivation or money to do it. Can you do it now? Can you do it today? Well, you cannot say you will do it tomorrow, as there is going to be no tomorrow.

In the earlier days, people used to spend their last few days with their family. All the relatives, children, close people and friends gathered and comforted the person who was going to die in a few days. They took take care of the person who was ill, cooked his (or her) favourite food, sang his favourite songs, talked to him, listened to what he had to say and made sure they did everything to make the dying person feel comfortable, so that he died happily. In those days, people believed that if a person dies happily then he stays blissful forever even after death.

In the modern world, people predominantly spend their last days in hospitals surrounded by doctors, nurses, tubes and beeping machines. If their condition is very critical, then hospital authorities won't let anybody inside to see them. Visiting hours will be strictly followed.

When you are surrounded by machines and complicated wires, are you aware how much time is left on your ticking clock? Do you know how many people are waiting for you outside? Well, what will be your last words? Whom do you want to say them to: your spouse, children, grandchildren or friends? Who is going to be around you during your crowning moment? What if you are dying in a hospital and all you are surrounded by are those machines and maybe the nurse who is taking care of you? Do you even know her name? If yes, what are you going to tell her?

What do you aspire to do? Have you given a thought to it? Each second, every passing minute, each and every hour seems to be very much valuable when you have very little time with you. You have no intension of wasting any single minute. You don't want to be lazy now. Do you want to sleep? Once you are dead, you have all the time in the world to do just that: sleep, sleep and sleep. You are not expected to do anything more than that.

Every day has twenty-four hours. We have 36,525 days to live. How many days have already passed by and how many more days are remaining? (Calculate them) Do you wish to lead life the same way that you always did? Well, if you are happy living like that, then no problem. But if you are not happy, then some things have to be changed.

Most of the time, people are worried about their lives. They may think, care and worry about you, but they cannot live your life. Don't do anything that doesn't make you happy. Value your time. You don't know what you got, until it is gone.

You definitely have a burning desire inside you and a big dream in your mind. What if there is no tomorrow? What if you die tonight? That big dream then stays just a big dream. Work towards your dream now, assuming that you are going to die by the end of the day. What are your best qualities? What is it that you love doing? What are the skills you want to master? If the world ends in the next seven days, what would you do? If you had all the time and money on earth, what would you do? What would you do if success is guaranteed? What would you like your family and friends to say about you on your funeral?

A wise man once said, "Dream like you are going to live forever and live as if you are going to die tonight." We must live everyday as if it is our last and one day we'll get it right. Only then will we realise the value of time and do what we really want to do. Only then we wake up early, do what we love to do, eat what excites our taste buds and not waste any time watching TV, sitting idle or loitering around. We talk to the people who matter the most and do something valuable, worthy and interesting. We live for ourselves and not give a damn about what others think and say about us. We must live our lives to the fullest. Do you want to die? Well, we really don't have an option, DO WE?

So, nobody has promised that we will have the exact same life, on the exact same planet again as we got one now. Give your best shot at life. Live everyday as your "Grand Finale!" *It's your life, make it large.* You never know which day is going to be the last day on earth; that is the revolving mystery of life. So what did you do today?

Stage 20

Death is just the Beginning...

Death is not an event in life. We do not live to experience death. Death may be some sort of new beginning to us.

- Ludwig Wittgenstein

For the regular people across the globe, death is an adjournment and pretty much the end of everything. But there are several people on this planet who believe that actual life begins once they are dead. I once saw a documentary called 'Taboo' in the National Geographic Channel; this documentary talked about a tribal group that presupposes that true destined life begins once they are dead. They have been following this belief for hundreds of years. They don't treat death as the end; they treat death as the beginning of a whole new level. Strangely enough they mourn at birth and rejoice in death.

These tribal people worship all through their lives, preparing for their death. Each night, they gather at a place in the jungle and set up a big camp fire. They then wear long white pieces of clothing, sing, dance, pray, shout and go around the fire. They treat life as an opportunity to prepare for their death and the life thereafter. This sounds weird, doesn't it?

There is another popular group of people who believe in a similar kind of theory. They are terrorists who engage in suicide bombing. These terrorists are brainwashed into thinking they are dying for a larger cause and that death would be a new beginning for them in heaven. So they end up sacrificing their own life, along with that of thousands of innocent people.

On September 11, 2001, a group of young nineteen terrorists hijacked four American passenger airliners; two planes crashed into the north and south towers of New York's 110-storeyed World Trade Center building, claiming the lives of more than 3,000 people, causing property and infrastructure damages of at least $10 billion. The third plane crashed into the Pentagon, the headquarters of US Defence. The fourth plane crashed into a field, while the passengers were fighting against the hijackers.

On November 26, 2008, a gang of ten terrorists, all in their early twenties, attacked a boat of Indian fishermen in the Arabian Sea. All were trained assailants whose hearts turned into stone that showed no mercy on anyone. Eight places in Mumbai were attacked with AK-47 guns, hand grenades and bombs. More than 200 people were killed and 500 were injured in these attacks in Mumbai. Out of the ten gunmen, nine were subsequently shot dead and one was captured by the security force. He was later hanged (he had eighty-six charges across a 11,000-page charge sheet) on November 21, 2012.

Are all these terrorists who died for the sake of religion in heaven now? I honestly don't understand the logic of these suicide bombers and terrorists. How can they expect to go to heaven by slaughtering thousands of innocent people? Will God forgive them and bless them for assassinating innocent people? Will God appreciate them for reducing world population and solving the problems of religion? Will God ask them to join him in a party to celebrate the loss of lives?

Do these terrorists believe that God is eagerly waiting for them in heaven? Do they think by killing innocent people and themselves, they can stake claim to a private resort with a heated swimming pool in heaven? Are these terrorists going to get a royal treatment in heaven for their unexplainable magnificent sacrifice?

I think there are better reasons to fight for and die for than dying for the sake of religion. The death of terrorists isn't going to fix the problems of religion, which according to me don't even exist. How does the killing of thousands of innocent men, woman, children and themselves solve anything? How is it a solution to the problem faced by religion? Which God will be happy to see the deaths of so many of His own innocent creations? If He is thrilled by this, then He isn't God at all.

To believe dying and killing for religion is such a dumb, moronic and laughable logic. Well, the only people who believe in this are the people who train and brainwash these terrorists. Their only job is to train these terrorists; they are never going to indulge in any of the suicide bombing activities themselves. They play the game safely, without even getting into the ground. There is no risk for them at all; they don't have to sacrifice their lives. They too know that none of what they are telling others is true; they know too well that everything is a fantasy and a myth. But their words are so powerful and manipulative that young minds blindly believe what they say to be the truth.

How is it possible to be convinced about something we don't see or know and are not sure of? How can anyone blindly trust what others say? Yet, some people brainlessly believe what others say over and over again. When you hear a lie many times, it starts to sound convincing. Eventually, the lie becomes the strong, unshakable TRUTH! The worst part about this particular blind belief is you have to spare your life to see whether it is true or not.

Going back to the tribal people who wait for death, what is the guarantee that the life they have been waiting and preparing for exists at all? And if it exists, will it be better than earthly life? Where are they going to send them? To the planet Jupiter?

We may think that what the tribal believe in is so lame and dumb, but for them our lives may seem a hoax. According to the tribals, they are actually doing the right thing. Who is right and who is wrong? Is there really a dedicated planet for the dead people to live happily? Is waiting for death and entering a new place worthwhile? Or are we better off decaying on earth and becoming good manure to the plants here? In either case, we first have to die. There is no other way to understand this. Is death really a new beginning for mankind?

STAGE 21
WHAT AM I FEELING RIGHT NOW?

I am not afraid to die;
I just don't want to be there when it happens.

- Woody Allen

Ever since I started writing, I have entangled myself in a lot of thinking and reading. I constantly imagine what it takes to be dead that in my subconscious mind lies a constant question: what if I die tonight? What if this was the closing day of my show on earth? Then what would happen to this book? Who would continue this book? Will anybody show any interest to continue writing it and eventually publish it on my behalf? Who will even read it? What influence would this book create on the world? Will my book just lie somewhere out there without anybody noticing it? What if somebody sees it but they don't give any serious thought to it? What if no one cared?

I don't want to die though. Well, who wants to die? Even the people who want to go to heaven don't want to die to get there. After all, I am a human being. I too have the desire to live and complete this book. I desire to publish this book someday. I really hope to be alive till the day I make it.

Well, who knows which is the last day of my life? Does anybody know when their last day on earth is? There is absolutely no warranty or guarantee to life. Life is like the 'Made in China' product; we can never predict when it will stop working. The other thing that is happening to me after I started writing this book is no matter who I see or talk to, there arouses a thought in my mind sub-consciously: "Oh my God! He or she is going to die one day."

All the people I see around me on a daily basis are going to die. It's just a matter of time. I don't know whether it is strange to feel this way, but that is the truth, right? Sometimes, I can't believe that we have to die one day, leaving behind every single thing and this beautiful world. Do we have to die? Seriously? Unbelievable, yet true!

Life comes with an expiry date but no one knows the date. Any day could be our last.

Once there was a survey across the world. Around 1,000 people were asked whether they wanted to know exactly when and how they would die. About ninety-six per cent of them said they didn't want to know the truth. I fall in the remaining four per cent category. Wouldn't it be sensational to know when and how we are going to die? The results may be shocking and tragic. But if we knew we would die in an accident, can we avoid dangers that may cause accidents?

We are so confident about our lives. We believe we will definitely wake up alive the next morning that we set the alarm for the next day before we go to bed. Wow! That's a giant leap of hope and faith.Well, but do we know which alarm is going to be the last? We may die tonight. Okay. I am just kidding.

Well, there is always a little truth behind every 'just kidding'.

Stage 22
Who is to Blame?

Some people are so afraid to die that they never begin to live.

- Henry Dyke

Every day people are born and people die.We know what is the origin of our birth and how we are born. But we have little or no knowledge about death and its incalculable boundaries. Is there anyone rolling the dice of life and death? Who can we point our fingers at? Can we blame God for natural calamities such as earthquakes, floods, tsunami and hurricanes? Can we denounce nature for causing so many deaths? Is there any specific way in which life is designed to work?

Let's put it in a simple way: a car crashes into a truck and someone in the car dies. Now, what do the relatives of the person normally do in this situation? They may beat up the truck driver black and blue, make him pay for the damage he has caused and the life he has killed, send the driver to jail and get a good sum of insurance money from the car-maker and the person who died in the accident.

In another scenario, let us assume that a person has died after a minor surgery due to the doctor's mistake. His family may yell at the doctor and file a case against him and the hospital. If their lawyer is good, the family may win the case. They may send the doctor to jail, shut down the hospital for its irresponsibility, get a huge sum of money from insurance and also get a huge compensation from the hospital, riding on the sensation the case has created on social media and the entire nation. People may already be protesting against it!

Whatever the situation is, the dead cannot be brought back to life again. Once dead, always dead. Death is not a soap opera or serial in which people magically come back to life after thirty-three episodes. Sometimes in serials, the dead reappear in just three weeks, after a plastic surgery. Well, reality is not an Indian TV serial.

Regardless of how death occurs and the reason behind it, no one can be held responsible for it. No one can be blamed for it. No matter how much we complain and blame others, ultimately there is no use. If our time comes, we have to go. It is as simple as that. Some people believe that everything is written down with invisible ink on our foreheads. Destiny decides when, where and how we are going to die. Another set of people believe that death is just an event, it can come anywhere at any time.

Let me tell you a small story that I had heard in my childhood at a church sermon. It makes me laugh even today. I don't know about you though.

In a village, there lived a husband and a wife. They had a son and a daughter. One day, the husband died. The wife yelled at God asking him why He did such a miserable thing to her family. Her husband, children and she were very religious, they prayed to God every day. Why did God take her husband's life and put his wife and children in such a terrible situation? She shouted to God that He should have taken her life instead of his. She was so sincere and scary in her prayers that God had no option but to appear before her. He told her that He was capable of bringing her husband back, under one condition.

The wife jumped with joy on hearing this. At the same time, she was also curious to know what the condition was. God told her, "Madam, just like you wished in your prayers, you have to sacrifice your life in order to bring back your husband's life." The woman realised that God wasn't kidding with her. She was shocked. Slowly regaining conscious, she said, "No, no, no… you are God! If you want to bring him back to life, bring him back. I can't sacrifice my life for him."

Sadly, this is how life works. How much can a person love you? They may love you for a long time, but is there anybody willing to die for you? Are you ready to sacrifice your own life for the one you love with all your heart?

Nodding and saying 'yes' is easy, but if the situation presented itself, not many would volunteer to die. Nobody wants to sacrifice their life for others. Why would anybody do that? What benefits do you get by sacrificing your life for others? Money? Name? Fame? Create history? What else are we going to get by sacrificing our life for others? Well, does it really matter what are we going to get? Regardless of what we are going to get, if we sacrifice our life in the process, then what is the use of having anything and everything else?

Yes, there are people who risk their lives for others. They are soldiers, freedom fighters and bodyguards of highly successful people and politicians. They are extraordinary people. Normal people don't even think about it. Can we really expect someone else to die in our place? If they can die for us, then why can't we die for our own self?

Stage 23
Is it God? is it Nature? is it the Law of Life?

Take care of your life and God will take care of your death.

- George Whitefield

In India, it is exceedingly offensive and marginally illegal to talk and raise questions about God. Any talk on God ends in controversy. We can never discover the truth or arrive at a conclusion. Some questions are exceptionally entangled; they have no answers at all. Maybe they don't want to or they don't have answers. Certain religious people don't even entertain questions on God. People prefer sweet lies over the bitter truth.

In India, we don't treat God as our friend. We aren't God-loving people, we are God-fearing. We speculate that the creator sits on a gigantic throne and has the authority to do anything and everything His heart desires. We believe if we worship Him, He will do what is righteous and we will go to the promised land of heaven once we die. What if we don't pray and worship Him? Would He hand us a terrible deal and would we unmistakably go to hell?

But why would God be so narrow-minded and biased? We are all His creations, right? Will God be terrible to His own creations? Will He take care of us only if we offer prayers to Him and praise him? I don't think so. God is fair and just. He would never do anything fallacious. We blindly believe that God is good only to those who go to the temple, mosque or church. No! God will shower His blessings on us even if we do not ask Him for it. That is why He is there. God is meant to do the authentic justice to everyone and never the unacceptable dreads!

Well, anyway the topic of discussion of this book isn't God, but death, so we need to look into every possible angle surrounding death. If God has the control over life, then He definitely has control over death too. That is what everyone believes or is made to believe.

On June 16, 2013, in Uttarakhand, a multi-cloud burst at a height of 12,600 feet above sea level caused heavy rainfall (375 percent more than the average). The rain lasted four days causing devastating floods, landslides and eruption of the Mandakini river. It also destroyed bridges and roads, leaving about 110,000 pilgrims and tourists trapped in the valley. More than 6,000 people lost their lives to the waters. The tidal waves destroyed everything in their path, flooding more than 3,000 villages. Even with such devastation, the Kedarnath Temple stood still with minimal damage to the structure.

Did God trigger this outrageous disaster? Why did God slaughter 6,000 pilgrims and keep the temple safe? Was the temple built to withstand the enormous forces of nature or God safeguard it? If He protected His temple, then why didn't He rescue his own people who had worshipped Him at the time of the incident? Why didn't He show any mercy towards his devotees? What wrong did these pilgrims do? They merely went to Kedarnath to offer prayers. Was God so overwhelmingly pleased with their prayers that He wanted them close to Him and gave them a DIRECT appointment with him?

People die from natural calamities such as earthquakes, floods, famine, tsunami, hurricanes, thunderstorms lightning. Is the Almighty behind all these natural calamities? Well, He has the ability and power to do anything and everything, right? Does God cause the natural calamities that lead to the death of thousands of innocent people every year? Why is He doing this to us? Well, if He is NOT doing all these, why is God not stopping all these? Is He not capable of stopping destruction and devastation? Or does He not want to stop all this? Is He unaware of all the things happening to His own people? Is He ignoring us completely? Are we all in darkness? Is He not bothered about all this? Does the Divinity have a plan behind all this or is He just throwing random surprises at us? Can God be held responsible for deaths due to natural calamities? Is it all the act of God? Is it really Him?

We all believe and trust that God is the creator of all life on earth. If God is the creator of life, then He is solely responsible for death too, isn't it? But why does God want to wipe out his own creations? Just to make space for the future generations? The earth should never be houseful, right? Where is all of mankind supposed to go if the earth runs out of place to live in? Man has found water and nitrogen in Mars. But the planet is still not suitable for existence and survival of life.

Did God create an end to life just to solve the issue of space? Or does He want us to relish life only for a defined period of time? Does He want us to return to where we came from? But where have we come from? Of course, our mother's womb, but we cannot go back there, right? What I mean is: where do we actually belong and where do we go after this show on earth is over? Do we return to the kingdom of God or are we promoted to the next level with extended benefits, less struggle and more happiness and peace of mind? What is the next level? Will we become aliens or any other intelligent life form in another planet in a new galaxy, far away from the earth? We never knew, we will never know.

Another thing that I don't understand is this: if God is really the director of life and death then why is He allowing babies in the womb, infants and small children to die? They haven't done anything to displease him. They barely know the difference between good and bad. They don't even know who God is. Then why is God not giving them a chance to breathe? God is supposed to be kind, fair and a good boy, right?

Why doesn't God prevent accidents? All vehicles in India contain a picture or idol of God in them. We do *puja* (a form of worship) to our vehicles to make sure nothing untoward happens. Then why does God turn a blind eye to accidents and freak shows? Why is He so quiescent when His own creation is dying in His presence? Is it because He loves some people a lot that He misses them so much that He wants them to be back as soon as possible? It is legitimately complicated. Am I going to be punished by God for saying all this about Him and am I going to hell?

Yes... No... Well, maybe...

Can God redeem us from dying? Regardless of the *pujas*, sacrifices and trips to religious places of worship, God cannot liberate us. It does not matter which church we choose to go to and how many candles we light. No God can unchain us from termination. He may extricate us from teething troubles, give us favourable health and a few more years to live, but He cannot release us from death. He may give us peace of mind and happiness, forgive all our sins, give us an astounding life, shield us against all odds, guide us, protect us and be with us at dark times, but He certainly will not prevent death. I guess even He is helpless when it comes to death.

Well, if you so wish to, you may pray for miracles. Who knows, miracles do happen. Go ahead if you think it is worth giving a shot. But you will realise the futility of the exercise soon. Trying isn't a crime, but you have to wait for the results. How long will you wait? If it works, good for you. You may get a chance to live for 200 years or even more. What is the number that you prayed for?

But the truth is: it is impossible even for God to stop the death of mankind. He may live forever but He doesn't give us that joy. If that happens, then we would become God, right? Death is independent; it comes with its own attitude problems. God cannot do anything about death, it has to happen. We have no other option but to accept this and deal with it. We cannot blame God for not preventing death. Nobody can live forever, except Him.

Maybe God decided that where there is birth, there is life, and where there is life, there is an end too. In another perspective, what if those who commit evil, crime and sins and those who get angry and jealous, lie, take revenge on others, steal, rob, fraud, cheat, rape, be corrupt, make black money, fight, kill and indulge in sexual abuse, child abuse and terrorism live forever? What would the world turn into?

Thank god, death is mandatory. Well, if God created life and death, He is in no mood to change the rules of the game now and let us live forever. Instead of praying to God that we live forever, let us pray that He makes us splendid human beings. Let us not ask Him to stop the rain; instead ask Him for a more durable umbrella. Let us not ask Him for fewer problems, instead ask him for the strength required to face problems. When you pray, do not beg. Demand what you want and prevail upon getting exactly the same and nothing else as a substitute. If God has the right to give us this life, then He definitely has the right to take it back. What starts with God has to end with God.

Well, now that we have discussed the possibility of God and what He can and cannot do, let us now look at nature. I am not here to make any assumptions and predictions. I am going to just evaluate the possibilities. Of course, we do not know what or who is exactly behind everything.

Mother Nature is the source of all the things that we see, hear, feel, touch, experience and undergo. She gives us oxygen to breathe, food to eat, light, warmth and energy. Nature showers rains that help the crops grow. We drink water from nature's river.

Okay, I hear you. We drink water from the filter. But is your water filter creating the water? Water has to originate from nature. It has to flow through the mountains and rivers, before it finally reaches us. Nature is the ultimate source of everything. We human beings aren't capable of creating a single grain of sand, a tiny leaf of a plant or a drop of water. We take everything from nature, modify it and use it according to our needs. We cannot create anything, but we can destroy everything.

Nature has total control over human beings. Every day the sunrises, there is morning, afternoon, evening, the sunset and then there is night. This happens every single day without fail. The sun doesn't take sick leave or go on a holiday; he has been punctual every single day for the past 4.55 billion years. Nature has it all. Nature decides when to shower rains, when to snow, in which direction the wind blows, what happens when the earthquake strikes or the tsunami erupts and how many people will die. The human being has no control over the laws and forces of nature.

On April 25, 2015, an earthquake of magnitude 7.8 struck Nepal. It lasted for just fifty seconds but killed more than 9,000 people, injured more than 23,000 and damaged around 35,000 houses. It destroyed property worth five billion dollars and destroyed the whole city of Kathmandu. Thousands of survivors were rendered homeless, with no food, water, medical and sanitary help. Entire villages were flattened. Aftershocks struck with another earthquake of magnitude 6.7 on April 26. Yet another earthquake happened on May 12 with a magnitude of 7.3. More than 250 were killed and 2,500 were injured in this aftershock.

Can Mother Nature be held responsible for this earthquake that killed many of her own innocent children? Why is she doing this to her children? Is she doing it to maintain the harmony, rhythm and balance in the ecosystem? We human beings hurt nature in many ways. People dump garbage everywhere. Factories let poisonous gases in the air. They also let out highly toxic contaminated liquid in the water bodies, causing water and environmental pollution. This results in an increase in global warming. Human beings also cut down trees, build homes, buildings, bridges and skyscrapers. Day by day, we destroy nature more and more. Nature too has her limits. She gets enraged and fights back to show how powerful and capable she is. When Mother Nature cries, everybody is helpless.

Everything we get is from nature, everything exists because of nature, and ultimately everything belongs to her. Mother Nature doesn't expect anything in return from us. Everything was once free on earth. As we evolved and became civilised, we started pushing the boundaries of nature. *Whatever inside this line belongs to me, if you need something, you need to pay me money!* Human beings are the only species on this planet that pay money to live on earth. The earth is still free of cost for the animals, birds, insects, reptiles, plants, trees, mountains, oceans and marine life.

We have been exploiting nature for our survival for a long time. Nature has the authority over everything; she is the queen, the boss. Nature has created life and she decides when it will be taken away from us. She doesn't treat the rich and the poor differently. In her eyes, everybody is equal. She brings death to each one of us. She does not show mercy to the good or bad.

Nature always decides the good, bad and evil and life or death for human kind. Nature has total control over the animal kingdom, birds, insects, virus, bacteria, plants and marine life. Nature defines every creature's destiny. Nature creates life, nature controls life, and sometimes nature shows her rage in the form of earthquakes, heavy rain, thunderstorms and tsunami. These result in death in large numbers. We cannot fight against the laws of nature; she is more powerful than all the human forces combined.

Can Mother Nature be held responsible for natural calamities?

On December 26, 2004, an earthquake struck the west coast of Sumatra, Indonesia at a depth of thirty kilometres below sea level, with a magnitude of 9.1 to 9.3, triggering a series of devastating tsunamis with waves up to 100 feet high. They ruptured over a length of 1,300 kilometres at a speed of 10,000 km/hour, swallowing every single thing in their path. A total of 2,30,000 people were killed in over fourteen countries as a result. The total energy released was more than 1,500 times the energy that the Hiroshima atomic bomb released. This was the third largest earthquake ever recorded in the seismograph. It was one of the deadliest natural disasters in recorded history.

Who caused this devastating tsunami? God or Mother Nature? Who has the authority over life and death? Is it God? Is it nature? Both? Or is it some other higher authority? Who decides a person's death and how is it executed? Who can reveal the entire original mystery that revolves in and around life and death? Is it all pre-written? Is it meant to be? Is it destiny? Is it written in the stars? Is it decided at the time of birth? Who decides how long we will live and when we will die? Do we die in a random space and time with absolutely no terms and conditions? Are we allowed to read the terms and conditions of our death before we die? Or Do we just skip them without even having a look, like what we do when installing software in a computer?

What exactly happens after we die? Are we allowed to know what happens? Nobody has prior experience in death. So no one can tell us what it is to die. I mean we all are fresher's while we die. Is death something higher than life? Is death the destiny of life? The way each one exits life on earth may be different, but the result is always the same: death. So, who the hell is behind death? Is it God? Is it nature? Or is it the Law of Life?

Stage 24
What If... Suppose?

Millions long for immortality who don't even know
what to do with themselves on a rainy Sunday afternoon.

- Susan Erta

(**Warning:** Wearing the seat belt is highly recommended for this chapter in particular.)

Almost all of us, right from our childhood, are brainwashed into believing this: if we are a honourable human being, lead our life in a respectable way, do the right thing to all people, commit our life for the sake of social service, help the poor and the needy, feed the hungry, take care of the sick, give hope to the broken and stay by our family and friends during times of need, then we will directly go to paradise, where there is no misery. There is only ecstasy and happiness in paradise, with unlimited supply of food, bread, honey and milk. We have been told that we will fall in love with the interior design of heaven, which is a beautiful place right next to God, and that we deserve a place in it, as we believed in Him, worshipped Him every single day and night without fail, did a lot of infinite sacrifices and went to the temple, mosque or church without fail. By doing all this, we have gained an immortal life in heaven.

Congratulations on making it to the final destination you waited for all your lifetime!

On the other hand, if we don't live our life doing all of the above, if we live for our own self, show no compassion to others, commit sin and take revenge, then we will be thrown in hell, where Yamaraj would curse, punish and abandon us. He may even fry and eat us along with beer.

Ufffff! Take a *Kit-Kat* break from this vicious cycle. 'What if… Suppose' there is nothing called heaven or hell. When we are dead, we just lie in our coffins and nothing exists thereafter, as they consistently promised us it will – IT WILL! And we have lived all our life believing that we would go to heaven after doomsday and live the peaceful life of a prince or princess. I am not questioning your religious ethics or beliefs. Even I wish there is heaven, since I have been told it is magical, beautiful, marvellous, majestic, city market and wonderful. If heaven is so wonderful, why would anyone want to be on earth suffering pain, poverty, job, depression and frustration? Who doesn't want to go to heaven? Everybody wants to go to heaven, but nobody wants to die to get there. But how else can we get there? Is there any shortcut, alternative, flyover, freeway, underpass, highway or bypass to heaven?

What I am exasperatingly trying to convey here is no one has an actual photo (whether of high resolution, censored or a blurred low quality) or a video clip of heaven to prove that it unmistakably, unquestionably and undoubtedly exists. People may assure us in writing with their signature that we would definitely go to heaven if we do good things and that hell awaits those who do evil. But what is the guarantee, boss? How can you be so sure that heaven and hell really exist? Should we blindly believe what people and books say?

Nobody who has died communicated to us in any form that he or she has reached heaven safely. No one sent an e-mail stating, "I have safely made it to heaven, pal. It was a good flight with slight turbulence. The airhostesses weren't really hot and sexy but the food was good." Not so far. It has never happened before and it won't happen in the future too.

Maybe heaven and hell are not technologically advanced like the earth, which has computers, internet and mobile phones. But if Charles Babbage, Graham Bell, Thomas Alva Edison, Isaac Newton, Nicola Tesla and Albert Einstein are in heaven, wouldn't they have made heaven a tech-savvy place by now? Who knows! Maybe one day we can talk to the dead using Skype! Are the dead not allowed to demonstrate their talents and use their brains for the betterment of heaven, in heaven?

Who knows what it is like out there? How does it feel to be dead? Who is going to take us to heaven? Obviously, we don't know where it is, which direction it is situated and where to start from. We can't book a taxi to heaven. Where will the cab driver pick us up from? The graveyard? Whom can we ask for directions? Our neighbour? Who knows how long he has been dead? What if nobody comes to pick us up? How long we are supposed to wait in our grave, expecting someone to come and pick us up? Forever?

Maybe heaven and hell is just another fantasy, myth or a puff of smoke. It is a belief that has been perpetuated for a long time now. People, especially the religious kind, may even get angry and start a rebellion if anybody questions the existence of heaven. Well, how do they know heaven exists? Have they seen it, at least once? They too have been fed on stories or have read about it in some books or their ancestors told them heaven and hell exist. Who told their ancestors this story? Again, their ancestors! For God's sake, who has seen heaven for real? Nobody. People have been spreading these rumours and fantasies for generations together now. Isn't there an end to all this? When will people start thinking logically and question the beliefs made up by someone long ago? We have been blindly believing everything for years. We are still passing the same information to our future generations and also one day ultimately die with it.

If we question religious people, they would be aghast and tell us, "How dare you ask such questions and doubt the existence of heaven? You will definitely go to hell for questioning heaven."

Oh yeah? They scare people that if we question all this, then we won't get a place reserved in heaven - **'IT SEEMS!'** So do these religious people decide who goes where? They try to convince us that we are wrong and they are right. Let's say we agree with them (for a while) and genuinely try to believe that heaven and hell exist. But when will we find out for sure that heaven really exists? If we want to see, feel and savour the bliss of heaven, we need to die first. There is no other way to know the truth. Religious people say with so much conviction that heaven exits. But we won't know if it is true or not till we are dead. So people say whatever they want because we won't be fuckin' alive to see if it is true or not. If heaven doesn't exist, there is no way we can blame the people, as we are not alive to do so.

Let us assume that we're dead, only to find out there is no place to go, then what happens? Well, what can we do?

What can we possibly do about it? Who can we blame for making us believe that there is a place to go after death? Whom can we ask this: where is the promised land of bliss? Can we lament that we did so much to please God and in the end we realised there is no such thing as heaven? Can we lament the fact that there is nothing out there except thick black darkness and pindrop silence? Can anybody hear you when you are trapped?

We can't ask anybody anything once we are dead. Can we blame ourselves for believing in all the mumbo-jumbo? I am not arguing the existence of God here. That is an entirely different topic for another time. The theme here is heaven, hell, immortality and what THEY say about all this! The question is not whether life exists after death. The real question is how alive are you before death.

Billions of people who once lived on this planet are dead now. Hundreds are dying right now, as you read this. Another billion people are not even born yet. Millions of them are yet just babies and thousands have just been born. But the thing is: all of them will die, there is no escape. It is the hard and indigestible truth of life.

The earth is pretty damn big; it is 12,700 kilometres in diameter. It consists of 7.3 billion people. The earth is 4.55 billion years old and human life has been traced back to thousands of years. How many billions of people would have been born, lived and died on this planet until now, altogether? Can we count that? Apart from the humans, there are trillions of animals, birds and marine life. We may not get the exact count, but let us estimate that 150 billion people have lived and died on this planet until now. Does heaven or hell have room for so many people? Does it have enough space for many more people who are still living and the people who are going to take birth in the future? What is the maximum capacity of heaven and hell combined? How many rooms are there? Won't it be congested with so many people? Won't hell be houseful as there millions of wicked people out there?

I have seen many people, mostly my friends, engage in plenty of sacrifices: they don't eat non-vegetarian food on certain days of the week, people go to temples, churches and mosques hoping that when they die, regardless of how many sins they have committed in their life, they would go to heaven and taste bliss. Can we do what we want to do and then go to God for pardon? Can we expect God to forgive us and accept our sincere humble apology? Will He reserve a seat for us in heaven? Will He welcome us in person when we get there?

We do not know for sure whether God has heard our prayers and forgiven us. We assume He would forgive us because we have done so many *pujas* and sacrifices and burnt a thousand candles. He never utters a single word of forgiveness or confirms that our prayers successfully reached Him. It is all in our minds to celebrate whatever we rely on. Does God expect us to bribe Him with money? He never asked us for any money. He also didn't ask us to make sacrifices, did He? Will He look after us only if we pray to Him?

We keep bugging God every now and then. Won't God be tired of listening to our problems, endless wishes and unlimited demands? We do the same things all over again. We go to God with a new deal every time. This is a never-ending loop. As they say, "Life is a cycle." And I guess God is in the centre of that circle. I think God is sincerely more pleased with atheists than the believers, because they don't bother Him at all for whatever reason.

No offence or defence meant, but sometimes I pity the vegetarians. All their lives they are made to believe that the greatest sin is to eat an animal – 'Veg,' that is 'NON,' 'Non-Veg!' Oh… My… GOD! There is no other sin, which is equal to or greater than this. If there is sin, then this is the only sin! If I think hard and dig deep into it, I realize that I don't legitimately understand the logic behind being a vegetarian. If you don't want to kill a life, then you must not eat vegetable, plants and fruits too. Even they have life. Just because plants don't have blood and they don't move, that doesn't mean that they don't have life.

If you cut and eat plants, even they are going to die. We should save the plants as they give us oxygen, keep carbon di-oxide at bay, maintain the balance and harmony in nature, reduce global warming and air pollution and provide us fresh oxygen to breathe. Animals don't help reduce global warming. They pollute the environment. Being human beings, it is our sincere duty to save the only planet that can sustain life. Take a pledge to go green and save our environment and planet.

Well, that's not the point here. I don't want to hurt your vegetarian feelings with my non-vegetarian feelings. What I want to convey here is this: if you have been eating vegetarian food all your life, you have never tasted non-veg. You don't know how tasty, juicy and yummy non-veg food is. That's sad. But wow! It is sincerely tough to be a vegetarian for life. Hats off to you guys! You are doing a great job with this big-time sacrifice. But, what if you are dead only to realise that there was "**NO RULE**" that you shouldn't eat non-veg. You could have eaten whatever you wanted all your life. But you were trained to believe that it is a sin to eat non-veg, even talk or think about it.

We humans commenced our journey on earth by eating raw meat by hunting animals. We ate animals for our survival. The first tools and weapons we developed were purely for hunting. Gradually, once we invented fire, we began to roast the meat and eat it. Eventually, humans moved away from the forest to the land and there was a scarcity of the animals. Then man developed agriculture and started eating plants and vegetables.

When did we change track? When did a bunch of people become vegetarians? I don't understand. Again, I am not being offensive or rude towards vegetarians. I am not trying to change anyone's minds to start eating non-veg. I am just asking what if this concept of vegetarianism was somebody's fantasy, thought or imagination, just like the concept of heaven? What I feel is: If one wants to quit consuming meat, then let him (or her) do it by his own wish and NOT because they are forced by some ancient beliefs, which is made up by someone centuries ago! Can the vegetarians live forever by saving all the other animals?

All this may sound silly, stupid or complicated.I don't know, even I am eager to see heaven, if it honestly exists. What if everything was a lie? What if everyone was lying to us all the time? What if heaven never existed at all and nothing is real? Did people make a fool of us? What if all this was somebody's fantastic imagination, which they thought was worth spreading? What if he or she felt that all this shit sounds pretty interesting, exciting and worth spreading? People don't think, they just believe. People scare other people and make them swallow anything. People could be "SINCERELY WRONG" sometimes! As Adolf Hitler says, "Make the lie big, make it simple, keep saying it, and eventually they believe it to be the TRUTH!"

This wasn't an attempt to hurt the feelings of the religious or the vegetarians. May be I am completely wrong. (I hear the vegetarians cry, "Yes, you are!") I am not talking with surety and conviction. I am just talking about the possibility of what it may be like out there, at the end of life. Don't think of this based on the current situation. If you do so, you won't get the answer right. Think of it as it is supposed to be, think of it from that dead-end perspective and you may possibly find the answer.

Apart from all this, in almost every religion, there is the concept of heaven and hell. If a Christian dies, will he go to the Christian heaven? Will a Hindu go to the Hindu heaven and the Muslim to the Muslim heaven? Where do the Buddhists, Sikhs, Jews and Jains go? Does each religion have its own heaven, spread across millions of acres, registered in the name of a particular religion? Or is it one big beautiful heaven, where there is no discrimination between religions or castes and everyone is treated the same. Are animals allowed in heaven?

What about hell? Are there distinct hells for different religions or they all maintained under a single roof? What about the sub-categories and sub-castes? India has more than 3000 castes! We humans are good at dividing and creating new categories. If each category has a separate hell and heaven, how many heavens and hells are out there?

In a whole new perspective, what if we are dead and taken to a kingdom where everything is sparkling white, angels fly all over the place and an old man, with a long white beard is seated on a mighty throne. You may have realised that the place must be the kingdom of God and the old man is none other than God himself. Yes, you are right, He is God. He asks you one question, "Son, how was your life of 100 years in heaven?" What could your answer be? "What? That was heaven? Nobody told me that was heaven, man! I thought it was just earth and we go to heaven after we are dead." What if earth itself is heaven and hell and nothing exists thereafter?

No matter what and how much I tell, how rude or offensive it sounds and what you believe in, you and I will find out the truth one fine day. But what if we never find out at all? How are we supposed to find out if we can't see, hear, think, say, feel or reason anything once we are dead? How are we even going to find out whether all that we were told and made to believe is the truth? What if we are not able to find out what was the truth and what was the lie? That would be so pathetic, man. Fingers crossed. Hope that never happens.

People may have come up with the concept of heaven and hell because human beings were busy doing evil to their own fellow men. So they may have imposed this concept of heaven and hell to ensure man lived life doing good and repented for all the sins he committed. People may have also tried to convince others that there is no escape from the prison of hell if they did evil on earth. On earth, people may be able to bail themselves out of trouble using money, power or influence. But there is no escape from hell. These concepts may have been introduced to motivate people to do good and lead a better life, free of crime. But as days passed, the concepts got so exaggerated and here we are today.

Gradually, people started thinking on these lines. They wanted to be happy even after they were dead. Isn't it way too much? They began to lead a good life and turned towards God with the quest to reach heaven and reduce the impact of their bad deeds. Many people continued their bad deeds and then went to God and asked for forgiveness. And again they did the same deeds. Won't God be tired of forgiving the same person three times a week?

People's demands are never-ending. They always want more and more. We don't pray to God; we just make business deals with him. We think that He is just sitting on a mighty throne somewhere far away only to grant us the things we ask for.

We all pray, but is He really listening to all the prayers and requests from billions of believers? How big are the storage spaces and servers in the kingdom of God to record and store all the prayers and requests? Who is maintaining all the information, prayer logs, unanswered prayers, pending requests and demands and questions? Are all our prayers in safe hands? Is all the data threat-and virus-free? Does God have a back-up of all our prayers? What if something goes wrong or someone hacks into those servers and all the data get stolen? Should we start praying right from the beginning? Oh no! We may have forgotten what we prayed for all these years! Nobody is going to hack into these servers, right? How often are servers updated for better and faster delivery? What kind of an algorithm has been written?

I am not writing this book to brainwash you, make you change your mind or disappoint you. You have strongly believed in something all your life. I cannot and I do not have the right to say you have been wrong and I am right.

Let me make this clear. Even I wish heaven exists. Let's meet up in heaven and have a lot of fun. I am not telling you to just believe what you read here or hear anywhere else. Before believing anything and jumping into any conclusion, positive or negative, ask yourself questions and use your reasoning power to judge and discern the right from the wrong and the good from the bad. As the Buddha says, "Believe nothing. No matter where you read it or who said it, even if I have said it, until and unless it agrees with your own reason and common sense."

It is up to you to choose what you want to believe in. Make a wise decision regarding your thoughts, the images you hold in your head, the things that you believe in and your expectations. Keep an eye on your expectations! Because in most of the cases expectations only end up hurting you. I was just discussing the possibilities and the scenarios "What if… Suppose?"

Stage 25
The Fantasy

Even death is not feared by the one who has lived wisely.

- Buddha

Death was always, still is and will always be a mystery, not only to mankind, but also to the animal kingdom, birds, insects and marine life too. There is absolutely no proof, record or valid explanation to explain what transpires in death and thereafter. The dead do not disclose their feelings; the dead cannot see, hear, feel, sense, smell, respond and react to any of the vicissitudes in their bodies and their surroundings. Death is out of our control, until and unless we opt for suicide or kill another person and become the decider of their death.

There are a thousand theories, beliefs, myths and stories regarding what happens after death. They vary across people, country, region, community, religion, race, family background and so on. But whose theory is the right one to rely on? There is no single theory, there are several of them. Is death the same to everybody or is it different for different groups and religions on earth? Many people have tried to explore and understand the world of the dead, but how far did those experiments succeed? Different people have different theories and answers. Which is the truth? No one knows.

The most religious people believe that if a person lives his life for the betterment of his people and society and is righteous to his family and community, then he will be placed in heaven and vice-versa. God is the deciding factor and He decides who goes where. Heaven is the place where God lives and there is unlimited happiness here. Hell is ruled by King Yamaraj. People get creative punishments for the sins they have committed on earth. Is hell a state-of-the art secure prison for the dead?

Another set of people believe nothing noticeable occurs after death. Our body stays buried, gradually decays and decomposes with the soil and becomes valuable manure to Mother Nature. If the body was burnt, then nothing remains other than a kilo of ashes, which is later dumped in the water. No one will pick it up and take it to heaven or hell.

Many others rely on the conception that if a person dies with an unfulfilled wish, he or she turns into a spirit and comes back to the earth to fulfil those desires. Once all their desires are fulfilled, the spirits are satisfied and they go back. I don't know where they go back. Do they go right back to where they came from? Where did they come from? Why do they have unfulfilled desires? Were they too busy doing unimportant things rather than fulfilling their desires? Why didn't they fulfil their desires when they were alive and had the opportunity do so? Why do they want to fulfil their desires once dead? Isn't it too late?

There are another set of people who don't know what may happen after death. They are clueless about what to believe and what not to. They are tenuous. They are happy if there is heaven and they find a place in it. They are okay even if there is no heaven or hell. They do not expect anything. Anything that they discover would be a surprise.

And finally there are those people who have not given a thought to what may or may not happen. They may not have the time to think or they may not want to think about what is going to happen after their death. They choose to live a life free from all thoughts. They presume that there would come a time to think about it and that time is not anywhere around. They live in the present.

Setting aside what we think or believe, one day all of us will find out the truth. One fine day, everybody gets a chance to die. Nobody is in a hurry to know the truth.The later the better.

After reading a lot, researching, thinking, analysing and writing about death, I have come up with my own fantasised version of what happens in the aftermath of death. We humans are gifted with the reasoning power to judge and decide what is right and what is wrong, raise the questions and find the answers.Well, who gave us these powers? God? Mother Nature? Or the Big Bang? It doesn't matter, as long as we have the powers. Now let us the step into my fun-tasy world of death.

There lies a huge spick and span world far away from the planet earth, the solar system and the Milky Way. It is known as the Valley of the Dead and Reborn. The valley is physically present somewhere in a particular space and time. The valley's existence dates back to the existence of the earth. In terms of sheer size, it is three million times bigger than the earth. It resembles the planet earth at large, with no specific scientific explanation and reason behind its formation. NASA knows nothing about this leviathan world, the Hubble telescope till date has never captured a single frame of this well-formed mammoth pulchritudinous world.

If humans managed to travel at the speed of light (300,000 km/second), then it takes just 100 lifetimes to get to this world. But God works in a mysterious way. There is a small, simple and an easy shortcut that would take us to this planet. It is death. It is a world where the dead are kept and they stay here for a long time. The crew of the *Interstellar* movie tried to find this planet, but failed.

The world is surrounded by greenery all around: a wide variety of trees, plants and singing birds, most of which are not found back on earth. The waterfalls soar from extravagant heights, gushing down tens of thousand gallons of fresh pure water from the mountains to the ground, every second. Mountains are fifty to hundred times taller than the Mount Everest. Oceans are twenty to thirty times larger than the Pacific Ocean, covering billions of square miles of fresh blue water. Enormous open grounds of green fields as far as the eye can meet. A constant source of natural light all the time, resulting in no concept of the night. Temperature is always constant: neither too high nor too low at any given point of time.

This world pretty much looks like how the fresh green earth looked like at the beginning of time, billions of years ago. It is untouched by humans in any way. There are no houses, buildings, skyscrapers, museums, vehicles, roads, airports, railway stations, public transport, banks, ATMs, shopping malls, offices, factories, industries, mobile phones, mobile towers, computers, robots, satellites or any other man-made things, inventions and structures. The valley hasn't undergone any human invasion. There is absolutely no technology here. It is a natural habitat. Instead of technology, this world has Mother Nature ruling over it.

The Valley of the Dead and Reborn is free from all kinds of pollution, global warming, junk, electromagnetic radiation, natural calamities, accidents, unemployment, war, poverty and hunger. All that exists here is peace, harmony, the spell of silence, the splendor beauty, the chirping birds and the roar of the raging waterfall. The valley is beautifully designed and perfectly engineered for all those people who are tired of living on earth and have reached their final destination. The only passport required to get to the valley is death. One has to die in order to get here.

Human beings, animals, birds and the fishes of the sea die at every stage of their lives. So the valley consists of people, animals, birds and fishes of all types and ages, irrespective of where they come from, what language they speak, what colour they are and what religion, race, caste, gender and community they belong to. Anything and everything that dies on the planet earth gets shipped to the valley and stays here nearly forever. Earth is one of the main 'clients' of the valley, with a contract that is up from billions of years and is going to continue for another billions of years. The valley is known for its uninterrupted error-free service, precision, perfection and attention to detail. There is no shutdown due to technical difficulties; there is efficiency, punctuality and non-stop operations.

The first man to set foot on the valley is believed to be Adam, as he was the first person to die on earth, followed by Eve. The two made a good couple and roamed freely on the surface of the valley. Gradually, more and more humans, animals, birds and marine life joined them. Now the valley is filled with billions of people. No matter how many people enter the valley, it will never run out of space, unlike the earth. There is always room for everyone here.

Once death occurs on planet earth, the dead become eligible citizens of this valley. There are no flight tickets, transportation charges, entrance exams, passport or visa. There is no customs or immigration clearance, security check, travel time, advance booking, reservation and baggage. What was owned on the earth must be left behind on earth at the time of departure to the valley. If anything is found in the pockets, such as keys, chewing gum, handkerchief, wallet or spare money, they are of zero value in the valley. Once dead, anybody and everybody are permitted inside the planet. There is no other known way to get inside the valley.

There isn't any inauguration, welcome speech, dance, prayer, briefing, special instructions, terms and conditions, security deposits and locker rooms. There is no need to stand in any queue, fill out any application form or submit any photo identity or address proof. People constantly flow into the planet. When two people enter, three people leave the valley at every ticking second. There are dedicated incoming and outgoing doors for humans, animals, birds and marine life.

Once people enter the Valley of the Dead and the Reborn, they are called 'valleyans,' not aliens. Even aliens have a separate place in the valley, placed extremely far away from the humans. Of course, aliens have life and they die too. Humans are not going to identify the aliens, as they never found them on the earth. Here in the valley, even the aliens are called valleyans and have the same rights as the humans and the animals.

The valleyans can communicate with each other in a single universal language known as Dythia. All the valleyans are treated the same way; all are equal.There is no concept of God, religion, caste, race, ancestors, rich, poor, money, the good, the bad or the ugly. There is no luxurious royal treatment for the good and punishment for the bad. The valleyans cannot bring any possessions into the valley nor can they take anything from the valley. They can't own anything or pick up something from the surface of the valley and say it is "mine."

As the valleyans are pure spirit souls in their native form, they don't need any food as they will never be hungry. They don't need any water as they don't feel thirsty. They don't need any air as they stopped breathing the moment they died. That is the reason why they are here on the valley. They don't need beds as they don't feel sleepy; back on earth their bodies were in constant sleep for 1,000 years. They don't have to earn money or pay any tax or money to stay on the valley, unlike on earth. Even though the valley looks and feels like earth, there are no rules and regulations and terms and conditions.

The valleyans are free to roam around anywhere and everywhere in the valley and can freely communicate to anyone they come across. But they have to first learn the valleyan language and adapt to it, similar to what they did on earth when they were born.

There will not be any memory of the past life. The life of all the years they have lived on earth will not be remembered. The valley gives a new beginning to the old end, providing people with a fresh start, in an astonishingly peaceful environment that feels like home, far away from home. Some claim to have glimpses of their memory but eventually everything will fade away. There is no place for the past in the valley.

The valleyans do not possess any emotion such as anger, jealousy, violence, happiness, love, hate, competition, sacrifices, sentiments, drama, dreams and passion. All they have is a peaceful spirit and soul that causes no harm. They are not forced to follow any specific set of rules. They have had enough rules imposed, followed and broken back on earth. They are not restricted from any part of the valley. There are no facilities such as computers, internet, mobile phones, GPS location services, Google, e-mail, WhatsApp, Facebook, greeting cards, letters or gifts. They are all on their own and are not ruled by any god, king, dictator or politician. There is no leader or follower. The valley doesn't discriminate between the rich and the poor.

The valleyans don't have to go to work and do a nine-to-five desk job. They don't have careers, family, possessions, house, cars, gold, property, criminal minds, desires, hopes and expectations. They don't have to get married and suffer. Everyone respects everybody; there are no enemies. The valleyans are put into the valley to prepare for their next life and forget all the things they have done and the disasters they had been through in their past lifetime.

The valleyans on an average stay in the valley for 100 years until their soul gets enriched and is ready for its next life's journey back to earth as a different living species. A human being in one life doesn't necessarily get to be a human being in his next birth too. He could be anything: animal, insect, bird, fish, reptile, bacteria or virus and possibly a human being too. It is up to the valley and the soul to decide which material body form it chooses to reside in, depending on how the soul was being treated in its previous birth, the current requirements and the need to maintain balance and harmony.

Once a valleyan completes his term and the soul is sent back to the earth, he or she doesn't remember any of the things that happened in his previous birth or in the valley. He gets a fresh start in life and everything begins from zero. He has to learn everything: crawl, walk, run and talk all over again. He may have been a scholar in his previous birth, but he won't remember a single letter or word from his previous birth.

This process has been happening from the very beginning of life and death. It will continue to happen in the same way in the future too. We are born on earth, life exists on earth, we live our lives on earth, we die on earth and we are moved to the Valley of the Dead and Reborn, back to where we came from. We all belong to the valley. This is our real home. We are here on earth for a maximum of 100 years and then get back to the valley.

No matter what life form the soul is put into, if it has a life, then it has its own purpose to serve: to live and let live. Life doesn't exist without any purpose.

The Valley of the Dead and the Reborn may or may not exist. I am not sure. It is a concept like the theory of heaven and hell. This is my fantasy creation. Who knows someone similar might have created the fantasy of heaven and hell! Who has seen what is really out there? People have said, written, believed and passed on their beliefs across generations.

The human brain is highly developed and is capable of creating, imagining and believing things that don't even exist. In fact, it is very good at it.

We all have our own reasons, logic, reasoning power and understanding. Before blindly believing what people have been telling you for generations together and jumping to conclusions, stop yourself. Ask yourself if it all make any sense. What happens after death and where we may go after death may be a fantasy, but life isn't a fantasy. We are blessed with the power to think and analyse and the opportunity to make a difference to the world and make planet earth a sweet and better place to live in. What else are we here for?

Stage 26
Is Life Worth Dying for?

As long as the body is healthy and under control,
death is distant; try to save your soul.
When death is immanent, what can you do?

- Chanakya

Life is priceless and precious, The healthier you are, the longer you live. Well, sound health doesn't prohibit us from dying in accidents, from natural calamities or being killed. Unfortunately, life doesn't come with a replacement warranty. The birds in the sky, the fishes in the sea, the animals in the wild, the plants in nature and the human beings have just one life.

Every single day sees the birth of someone and the death of someone else. Babies are born; they crawl, walk, talk, grow up, get educated, write exams, fall in love, work all their lives, get married, have kids, raise a family, retire and get old. What happens after that? We can pray, do our habitual nine-to-five desk jobs, run profitable businesses, pursue our dreams, make a lot of wealth, waste this life, believe in God or rely on science. Despite what we say or not say, whether we stay single or get married, what we do or not do, whether we live or merely survive, one day we have to stand at the edge of life and embrace darkness and pin our ears to the profound blackout silence, sniffing the fragrance of the euthanasia.

At times I wonder if life is really worth dying for. Why do we have to sacrifice our life? Why is there such a gruesome thing called death? Why do we have to die? Just to preserve the balance and harmony of the planet? To give a chance to the fresh upcoming talent? It doesn't matter how we came on earth, whether God gave life to us or the Big Bang created it all, either by choice or by accident. How? It doesn't bother us. The million-dollar question is: why is our life being taken away from us? If it is going to be taken away after a certain time, why did we come to the earth in the first place? What are we expected to do with our lives? Why are we here?

Is there some favour we can do to gratify death so that we can live forever? Can we play a game of chess with the Grim Reaper? If we win the game, will death go away and never come back?

It was a Friday, the thirteenth day of April 2015. I stepped out of the bus after a long tiresome journey of seven hours from *namma* Bengaluru. Pitch-dark midnight welcomed me to my hometown. I had to walk a distance of 300 metres to make it home. There was not a single soul at sight, not even a stray dog. With the moon on a holiday and the street lights burnt out, I switched on the flashlight of my smartphone to find my way home.

The silence was astounding. I heard the roar of a bus at a distance.

The wind began to gain speed, the trees started rattling and battling with the wind and thick black clouds slowly formed in the sky, covering the enormous heaven and swallowing the bright twinkling stars. Even before I could walk ten steps, Mother Nature turned on her shower. Rain is not a surprise in my hometown. It showers all through the year in any season for no reason. It was season's first rain and the mud smelled delicious. I wished I could taste the soil.

I took a step and a luminous white light dazzled behind me. I focussed on the illumination on impulse. There smacked a jolt of lightning from the vault of heaven. This was followed by a thunder, and a furious rainstorm paved its way from the clouds. The hypersonic light was immensely powerful. I couldn't look at it for more than three seconds. My flared eyes made me believe that there was a life form behind the light. A conflict arose in my brain.

Should I go home or go after the light?

I willed my mind not to react. All I wanted was hot coffee and gorgeous sleep. I took another step towards home. The light turned off and then it turned on again. This happened three times.

Was it a ghost? Was he giving me a signal? Well, I neither believe in ghosts nor am I afraid of ghosts. This was my hometown. I was in safe hands. I wanted to know what surprise awaited me. Without accepting defeat, I took a deep breath. I started walking towards the light, one step at a time.

Miscellaneous thoughts gushed through my brain. I could hear my heart beating like a wild galloping horse. My footsteps crackled against the dirt, the little stones and the splashing rain water. I came near the source of light. I began to get a glimpse of a human form.

He was well-built. Maybe seven feet tall. He was wearing a black full-length robe, a hood covered half of his face. A briefcase was on his left hand. There was a powerful light source, as bright as the burning afternoon sun, in his right hand. Judging by the appearance, he didn't look like he was in need of assistance. He seemed as though he was standing there with a definite purpose, as though he had been waiting for me.

I was just a few feet from him. He turned off the light. I stood still.

What the hell was I supposed to do? I wondered if I should run home. But having come so close, I wanted to try speaking to him.

"FUCK!!! You ran out of batteries, man?" I asked him for the second time, standing at an innocuous distance from him. There was no answer again.

"You got down from the bus? I don't remember seeing you in the bus."

His silence continued. All I could hear was the chatter of the pouring rain and a dog barking from a distance.

"Do you need any help, big boy? My house is just round the corner. You can stay…," I said.

He turned on the light and said in an authoritative voice, "I have been expecting you."

"I am sorry. Wh…whattt?" I exclaimed.

"You are writing a book, aren't you?" He sounded exceptionally confident.

I was stunned. Stammering I said, "Yeah. How on earth do you even know that? Who told you? (thinking) Are you spying on me? Are you a publisher or something? Well, you don't look like one."

"You have been writing a book about me; how can I fail to notice you?"

"Oh boy! I am afraid you are mistaken, sir. I am not writing a fairy tale about anyone. My book is abou—"

"DEATH!" he screamed and lifted his face, making eye contact with me.

I took two steps back in shock. I dropped my cellphone and my backpack. I just stared at his neon blue glistening eyes.

Stammering, I said, "Are you…"

"YES! Your majesty, you are right," he interrupted me.

"That means… My time is up? This… is this my last hour? This is it, uh? I am done?"

"No, no. It is not that bad. It is not yet time. You still have time… Sometime."

"Thank god," I thought to myself.

"Then… Then why are you here? To stop me from writing this book? I shouldn't publish it? Is that what you want?"

He looked up at the heavens and said, "Will you?"

Without a clue in my brain, I said, "Well, I am working very hard on this man. I mean, I really want to publish this book. Why do you want me to stop by the way? What is wrong in writi…"

"Did I tell you to stop?" he screeched, gazing into my eyes.

"No, I just assumed you wanted me to stop."

"I am here to help you. You seem to have some trouble finding the answers."

"Wow! Really? Can I ask you anything?"

"Anything," he said, with a generous smile.

He sat down. So did I.

The following is the conversation we had in the hours of darkness. It was a night to remember.

Me: What is your name?

He: My name is Grim Reaper, alias Death.

Me: Hmmm… When were you born?

Death: I was born when life came into existence.

Me: All right, sir. So when are you going to die?

Death: As I was born when primitive life form began on the planet, I am going to die along with the last life that dies on earth.

Me: That sounds promising. But why do you even exist?

Death: I exist to maintain the balance and harmony of the life cycle.

Me: That's it? Is it that simple? Oh boy! And I am writing a book on this?

Death: What's on your mind? What did you expect while writing the book?

Me: Uhhh… Nothing. You make a living from extermination?

Death: Yes. That is what I do and I do it best. It is my profession.

Me: Good for you! Do you forgive anyone… by any… chance?

Death: I have forgiveness towards no life in the past, present or future. I do not have the power of forgiveness.

Me: That's mean. What is your heart even made up of – stone?

Death: I have no heart. No hard feelings!

Me: Fine. Let it be your way! Do you treat everyone in the same manner? Regardless of religion, the God they choose to believe in, whether they are atheists, rich, poor, good, bad, rascals or the ridiculous?

Death: Unfortunately, YES!

Me: Great! Do you frequently visit heaven and hell?

Death: I am a realist. I don't believe in fantasies.

Me: Ahaan… Okay… There are several people residing on earth who dream, desire and believe in heaven. They are waiting and expecting to go to heaven. What is your claim?

Death: I wouldn't bother about it, if I was you. Each one has the authority to generate their own thoughts, definitions, logic, fantasies and judgments. It is up to every individual what they choose to believe in. I have never promised anything to anyone. My hands are clean, unlike their minds.

Me: Oh-kay! One important question: where do you reside?

Death: Interesting question. I am everywhere. I am the dark shadow of life.

Me: Fantabulous! Can you be more specific?

Death: Yes! I walk hand in hand with the living. I choose to stand, walk, jog, run, swim, fly and sleep with them. I watch every step, each move and every turn they take. I curiously wait for them to make that one wrong judgment. Then I capture them and there is no escape. Once they are mine, they stay mine forever.

Me: That's horrifying! Can you give me some relevant examples of the same?

Death: Don't you get it? I am with people when they are driving and crossing the roads – just inches away from them.

I hug them tight when they are on an adventure. One small wrong step for a man, a giant leap for extermination. I attack individuals in various forms of diseases. Heart attack is my all-time favourite. It makes my work a piece of cake. Accidents save my time and energy. Terrorists, serial killers and murderers work for me. Suicide invites me. I also swallow tens of thousands of people at the same time in the form of natural calamities. I am with people at all times when they are getting treated in the hospital, driving, swimming, smoking or drinking… You get the idea?

Me: That's scary! Do you work in some pattern or design of some sort?

Death: Yes, I do. I lay a set of traps on people's path and make the victim mine. Humans today have found methods to not fall for my baits. But I have new unimaginable ways to find my way through. I introduce new types of diseases. While human beings take hundreds of years to find drugs for the disease, I would already have digested millions of victims. The human being is a masterpiece; he always finds a way out. When he conclusively finds the key, I change the locks. I surprise them with even more abstruse diseases. Regardless of how long and hard man chooses to fight me, I will always be the winner. They may escape a few baits of mine, but in the long run, no single living has escaped from me, no one ever will. I conquer them all. Yes, there is a pattern and design for everything.

Me: That's clever and cunning of you. What is the popular response you get when you approach your victims?

Death: "I am not ready yet." This is the most common refrain from all my victims, regardless of their age, gender, nationality, God and religion. A few even say that the weather isn't good, it is a weekend, it is way too soon, they have a family and kids and so on. People come up with thousands of lame excuses if I allow them. So I have stopped listening to their senseless moronic explanations.

Me: Of course, no one wants to die. What do you tell them?

Death: I tell them they all say the same and that no one is ever ready to die! I don't entertain any excuses, emotions, begging or sentiments of any kind. I am sick and tired of them.

Me: So you don't even listen? Well, what bribe will you accept to set us free?

Death: Nothing! I won't set anyone free.

Me: That's bad. Does God have any sort of authority over you?

Death: You ask way too many questions.

Me: Why do you hold so many secrets? In order to get the answers, I need to ask the questions. Are you afraid to answer any further questions of mine?

Death: You better hold your tongue, you tiny living creature. I am not afraid of anyone or anything. Everyone is afraid of me. They poop in their pants when they see me eye to eye. You cannot frighten me with your questions, but my answers may scare you. What is your question?

Me: Okay chill. You don't have to scream, I am not afraid of you. Just answer my question, "Does God have any sort of control over you?"

Death: You're not scared of me? Time reveals the truth, my dear. It is easier said than done. Well, to answer your question, yes, I do consider His requests. But mostly, I prefer to make my own decisions, irrespective of which God the victim believes in and 'prays' to. I 'prey' them all!

Me: Are you a tough taskmaster like Hitler or do you possess a good sense of humour?

Death: I am neutral. Neither good nor bad, neither positive nor negative.

Me: Are you going to kill me? Are you going to kill every last one of us?

Death: Yes... Precisely!

Me: Hmm... Why are you hiding?

Death: I am not hiding from anyone. Do you wish to book an appointment with me instantly? Do you want to commit suicide? You can be right next to me in a blink of an eye. Go ahead! Do you want to give death a shot?

Me: That's ridiculous. Well, I am not in a hurry, big boy.

Death: No one is in a hurry. Some are slow, some are fast. It is just a matter of time, folks. You all end up in my kingdom.

Me: That's true. Well, are you an event or a journey?

Death: I am the journey of events.

Me: Is that a punch dialogue? Okay! Are you more attractive, jaw-dropingly fascinating than life itself?

Death: Come and see for yourself! You are always welcome. I never stop anyone from coming back home. The doors are always open for you and for everyone else too.

Me: I will. But... Hmmm...Why do people love life and hate death?

Death: That's because life is a 'beautiful lie' and death is the 'painful truth.' Their hatred doesn't bother me. When they had the opportunity to live, they wasted it. When I step in, they want to live; they start swearing at me. They promise to feed the hungry, take care of the sick, help the needy, change the world and all that routine crap! What the fuck were they doing all these days? Even if I let them live, what are they going to do? The same shit differently? And they hate me. Great! I am impressed. What more do I need?

Me: Hmmm… Relax. Cool down. Nobody is blaming you now for anything.

Death: Blame me? Who has the balls of steel to blame me? I am deaf to their blaming. They can only fight, merely compete, but can never win.

Me: Okay master! You win! Celebrate your victory. Be honest. Do you hate the living?

Death: No! I do not! I am just minding my business. All of you don't understand this. All this is merely a process. You first live, experience life on earth, then die, come to me and experience my world. I too have some attractive features and introductory limited period offers. I do not want to reveal any of them.

Me: Ahaaan… Okay. I will see you one day. Then I will know what you have on your menu. Now tell me, are you predestined or just a random event?

Death: Everyone must and should experience me. As I told you earlier, it is just a matter of time. Nothing is predestined. The living always die with a driving cause behind it. I don't execute anyone for no reason. You may encounter a deadly disease, accident, natural calamity, someone may kill you, or you may commit suicide. I don't have the direct authority to relinquish a life without any purpose, just like that. It all happens in a random space and time. There is no 'kick' if life and death are scripted.

Me: That's interesting. Once dead, can we meet the others who are already dead?

Death: I would like to keep some things as secrets, up among the stars.

Me: No doubt you would. I am just curious about what you have in that briefcase of yours?

Death: This briefcase? I give this briefcase as a gift to the dead when they come to me. This consists of the belongings of the dead.

Me: Belongings of the dead? You mean you'll have all my things such as clothes, money and stuff once I'm dead?

Death: Those things were never yours, they belong to the earth.

Me: Oh yeah! I got it, they are my memories, right?

Death: No. Memories belong to time.

Me: They must be my talents then?

Death: No. They belong to circumstances.

Me: No? It might contain my body then.

Death: No no… It belongs to dust.

Me: Seriously? Then surely it must be my soul! Don't tell me no.

Death: You are sadly mistaken. Your soul belongs to me.

Me: I am out of options. Well, does everyone get the same briefcase?

Death: Pretty much.

Me: I am not… de… dead yet, right?

Death: No, you are not. Why are you asking this? What's wrong with you?

Me: Just out of curiosity, that's all… Can I open and see the briefcase myself, even if I'm not dead yet?

Death: You are a prick, aren't you? Yes, you can. Here you go, it's all yours!

I took the briefcase from him and opened it, only to find it EMPTY!!!

Me: What? This is empty! Did you forget to fill it or… (stammering) I never owned anything?

Death: Option B. You never owned anything.

Me: Whattt??? Are you seriously serious? Then what is the point of having a life? What was even mine all along?

Death: Your 'moments!' Every single moment you lived was yours. Nothing else! Life is living each moment to its fullest. Life is just a series of moments. Think good, do good. Live it, love it or screw it. The moment is going to end… much sooner than you think.

Me: That was… something. I don't know. It's hard to digest all this. Well, is there any message you want to give to the living?

Death: Message? I would like to call it a warning. Do not underestimate the value of life, for it is only once you are laid with this opportunity! Wake up! Do not spend it as a slave under someone's feet, and worrying what the world thinks about you. Worry, envy and blame are such a waste of time. You can either stay a victim or take full responsibility of your life, accepting that you are the reason for every result you produce. All your past decisions have led you to where you stand today in life.

Every single soul is blessed with an equal opportunity. No man is greater than the other in any way. Unfortunately, greatness today is measured by the amount of money an individual owns. I do not judge, I do not consider money a factor. I treat the rich and the poor, master and the slave alike. At all times, develop your own thinking, watch your step. Stop thinking only about you, your stomach, your family and your world. Render useful service to the society, work for the betterment of mankind. Serve and protect. Find the purpose of your life and work hard with your blood and sweat to achieve it. Once you are dead, all you will be left with is nothing. Yeah, trust me, literally nothing! Except the deeds you did when you were alive. Value the time on earth because it is very limited, do not sit on it. Time is what life is made up of. Get up and get into action. For when I appear, I am going to destroy you – COMPLETELY!

Me: That was a formidable warning, your majesty. One last question: is life really worth dying for?

Death: Did you know whether life was worth living for before you were born?

Me: No.

Death: Then how will you know whether life is worth dying for, even before you die?

STAGE 27
WE DIE ONLY... TWICE!!

The life of the dead is placed in the memory of the living.

- Marcus Tullius

Metaphorically speaking, we do not die once, we die twice. Confused? Allow me to retort. First is when we physically die and the second death happens when the living people forget our name completely, forever. They say the dead are not in fact dead until and unless others choose to forget them. According to a survey, an ordinary person is remembered for a maximum of 75 years after his death. After that, his name barely exists, if he isn't a part of history. Do you know the name of your grandpa's grandfather, your great grandfather?

There are a million ways to stay alive even after a person physically dies. Take for instance some of the famous personalities who are dead. Why do you think people still remember them even after years? Some of them are remembered even hundreds and thousands of years after their demise. All those great people have observed, explored, explained, identified, experimented, discovered, created, invented, modified, improvised, developed, innovated, wrote, fought for or did something outstanding that made a huge difference to the world. All of them achieved something phenomenal in their own fields, creating an impact on millions of people. They made the world a better, easier, simpler and a safer place to live in. They too were once ordinary men and women, just like you and me. But they had a big crazy dream and the dedication and courage to achieve it. The results of their actions are what we see and use today: computers, mobile phones, internet, technology, inventions, vehicles, buildings, rockets and every tiny little thing. Everything was invented or discovered by man. They weren't a miracle of any sort. They were the result of pure dedication, sweat and hard-work.

Most of us won't be alive in the year 2100. (did that hurt?) But until which year do you want to be remembered? Just till 2133? How many people do you think would remember you and for how many days or years? People are not really worried about the dead. They talk about them for two to three days or a week at the most. And that's it! Kabooom! Then they have better things to worry about. After a few days, nobody even misses the dead. It was as though he or she never existed. That's the reality. That is the truth.

I read these inspiring lines somewhere:

"If you want to be remembered even after you are dead, then either write something that is worth reading or do something that is worth writing."

Was I inspired by this quote? Definitely! Not only this quote, there are thousands of other things that have served as an inspiration for this book. We can do good to people, a group or the community, we can invent something valuable, find a solution to everyday problems, work for world peace, eradicate poverty and hunger, provide good quality education, work for a pollution-free environment, save the nature, become a prime minister or a president, a good director, sportsman, the wealthiest man on the planet, and many other things, so that we are still remembered in the year 3333.

History is not only made up of people who influenced and changed the world. Adolf Hitler, Osama Bin Laden, Saddam Hussein and Veerappan are also a part of history. People still remember them. Not be in a positive way but yes, people do remember them. To stay alive in people's memory, we can even do bad things. We can destroy the world, kill innocent people and commit crimes, robbery, fraud and so on. Well, I don't want to give you any more evil ideas. History is replete with both good and bad people.

Someone once told me: if you want to be remembered even after you are dead, then take a lot of loans and debts and then die. The people whom you owe money will remember your name until they die. It is up to every individual how they want to be remembered. Do you really want to be remembered or do you want to die as just another ordinary human being? Make life worth living that one day your absence feels like a huge loss to at least a few people.

Do you have the potential to change the world and make the earth a better place for the future generations? Our chances of dying keeps on increasing day by day. Time is running out fascinatingly fast, babe and dude! Yesterday is already gone and there is no refund of time. Today will turn into yesterday and tomorrow will turn into today. What have we done with our life, all these days?

However life has been so far, we still have a chance to change it. It is never too late to start. Better late, than never. We are never too old to dream a new dream or set a new goal. We can always refine, reinvent and rediscover ourselves. We won't be recognised for what we said, thought, read and dreamt or where we studied, which degree we earned and where we worked. We are enshrined only for what we did. What help did we render to others, the society and the community? What difference did we make in other people's lives?

We have to be very careful about the words we speak, as words once spilled cannot be taken back. Be very careful when you decide how and with whom you spend your time? Because you are not going to get that time again. Do not be afraid of the people who are willing to hurt you. Don't take life too seriously, because you are never going to get out alive.

Go and live a life that you always wanted to. Let there be no regrets at old age about the things you could have done while you were young and when you had the time and energy. Let us regret the things we have done, rather than regret the things that we haven't done. Make a difference and be remembered. The first death is not under our control; the second death is completely under our control. Die only once, not TWICE!!

Stage 28
Death as I Saw it...

To a well-organised mind, death is the next great adventure.

- J.K Rowling

In the quarter of my lifetime, maybe a third or even half of my lifetime, I am not too sure how long, I have seen many deaths. The death of family members, friends, neighbours and strangers. Every death had certain things in common: loss, pain and tears. But there is one death in particular that is permanently smacked in my brain, which inspired me to write this book. Unfortunately, I cannot call it a special one; I would rather call it as an unforgettable death.

It was a just another delightful Tuesday evening on September 29, 2011. Some of my friends and I were returning from a picnic. We had been to a river side, 130 km from *namma* Bengaluru. We had a tremendous time from morning to evening with loud music, laughter and chatter. We had a great time making fun of each other. We drove back at a decent speed of 80 kmph as there was enough time for us to reach home.

Suddenly, a car overtook us at probably a speed of 100 kmph. So we picked up pace and overtook him. He overtook us again. And we drove past him in retaliation. This happened a couple of times. Neither the fellow car driver nor my friend who was driving the car was ready to give up on this ferocious race.

At one point in time, the competition was intense. Everybody in our car felt things were getting out of control. It was moving at a speed of 130 kmph. It was a single road with no divider in between. We told our friend to quit racing and drive normally as the speed was out of bounds. But he didn't listen to us.

We shouted at him to let the fellow car driver go his way. Both sides of the road were surrounded by water. But our shouting only stressed him out and he tried to speed up, instead of slowing down the car. But luckily the car wasn't going any faster.

As our friend tried to overtake the car ahead of us, we saw a car coming from the otherside of the road. Our friend had no other option but to steer the car to the left. At a speed of around 120 kmph, the car hit a cement bar that lay on the road and there was a thunderous bang. The car flew off the road, rapidly rolling to the left in the air. I was watching from the front windshield, counting one, two, three, four, five... And I was praying that the car would stop. Then there was pindrop silence. I thought it would be the last moment of my life. The car finally landed with a thud, upside down on the water. All the water on earth seemed to flow into the car. I still don't know how I managed to come out of the car and help two of my friends trapped inside to get out of the car.

I looked at the banks of the river. I saw my friend Ravi bleeding from his head, hands and body. He was almost covered in blood. He had somehow managed to reach the banks of the river. I turned my head to see the road on which we were driving; 100–150 people had gathered by then and they were staring at us. At that moment in time,

I didn't understand two things: from where did so many people come from and why didn't nobody bother to help us out of the car?

What happened in those nanoseconds? Everything was a mess! What were we supposed to do? My friends and I rushed to Ravi and carried him to the shore. We met two guys who helped us take Ravi to the nearby hospital.

The accident had happened in a small town. We rushed to a small clinic and gave Ravi basic first-aid. But the doctor told us to take him to a bigger hospital, which was 25 km away in *namma* Bengaluru. Without wasting any time, we started to the big hospital.

Ravi was lying on my lap. He was crying in pain; he was bleeding all over. I was constantly trying to calm him down. I repeatedly said that it would all be over soon and we were on the way to the hospital. I wanted to inform Ravi's parents, but he was strongly against it. He hadn't informed them about the trip and he refused to give me their mobile number. It took us forty-five minutes to reach the hospital.

At the hospital, one of my friends managed to get hold of Ravi's phone. He called up his parents and told them about the incident. They started for the hospital immediately. After an hour of treatment, the doctors told us to shift him to the Nimhans Hospital as they didn't possess the necessary advanced equipment in their hospital. Ravi had suffered injuries on his head. I had heard of Nimhans Hospital. It was a renowned hospital. We didn't have much of a choice and had to move fast. We rushed to Nimhans.

Nimhans was in the heart of the city. It took us more than an hour to reach the hospital, after being stuck in a terrible traffic jam.When we reached the hospital, I was given a big application form to fill. Patient details, I was told. As though the formalities were more important than a person's life! I remembered a similar scene from the movie *Munna Bhai MBBS*. Finally, all the formalities were completed and the initial treatment started. I had lost my mobile phone in the accident, so I couldn't contact anyone at that point of time.

As the nurses cleaned Ravi's wounds, wrapped bandages around them and hooked him to intravenous glucose, there was blood all over the place. Ravi was wailing in pain. I hovered my eyes across the emergency ward, only to find many patients in Ravi's condition. Some were even worse. People all around were howling in pain, some were praying, a few were silent and a few others were sleeping. Everyone around seemed helpless. Nurses and ward boys were in a hurry, rushing and running all around. Some carried reports and medicines and many had glucose and blood bottles.

Everyone was bothered, worried and lost. There was pandemonium all around. Some had broken bones and fractured hands and legs while some had injuries on the head and bandages all over the body. Some were bleeding badly. It was a dreadful and horrifying scene. The yelling in pain was unbearable. I could literally sense the smell of survival. Everyone was in pain, suffering and struggling for life. Within a few moments, I was lost in the chaos. The hospital is a very bad place to be in. I really don't understand how doctors and nurses deal with these things every single day. I couldn't take it even for a few minutes. I stood powerlessly, staring at the ceiling and wondering, *God! Are you really watching all this from above?*

In the midst of all this, I was called in for a formal enquiry by a guy sitting with a big register. I wondered why the register was so fat. As I sat down, he started firing questions at me. The way he was questioning me, it seemed to me as though he didn't believe it was an accident. Probably at the back of his head, he was treating it as an attempt to murder.

I told him clearly that it was an accident and we didn't cause any harm to Ravi. But he didn't seem convinced that it was an accident. He was surprised that my friends and I suffered no injuries in such a fatal accident that had caused so much trauma to Ravi. I told him that we didn't attempt to kill him. If we had tried to kill him in the first place, then why would we bring him to the hospital, I argued.

He stared at me for two to three minutes. I didn't speak a word, neither did he. I then broke the silence, "Can I go now?" But he had more questions. He wanted to know every tiny detail about the accident. Where it happened? How it happened? At what time? How do I know Ravi? How many people were in the car? Who was driving the car? Which car? I answered all his questions. He took my phone number, my personal details and my signature on the big fat register. He finally seemed to be convinced as my answers were consistent and confident. I didn't take too long to answer. Nor did I pause or stutter. He gave permission for further treatment from a doctor. Till then only the nurses were treating him.

Then the doctor came and started treating Ravi. Seeing the reports, he too started asking the same questions that the inspection guy had asked me. I answered him patiently and also told him that Ravi's parents were on their way to the hospital. The doctor told me that Ravi was fine. There was no risk to his life, though he would need three to four months of bed rest. But he was out of danger. This was a big relief.

We had to pay the bills till then before more treatment started. Ravi's mother and his cousin reached the hospital by then. Ravi's mother was crying continuously. I explained to her everything that had happened and what the doctor had told us. I then went away to pay the bills.

Since I hadn't taken a visitor's pass on my way out, the guard wouldn't let me inside the emergency ward again. There were fifty to sixty people begging him to let them go in. The emergency wasn't only for me; it was for everyone. The guard didn't seem to appreciate anybody's emergency. He experienced this situation every day. His job was to keep people away from the emergency ward. It was just another routine day at work for him. I didn't even have my phone to call my friend who was inside. I waited for about twenty minutes at the gate, recalling the accident. How did such things happen?

I somehow managed to get near the gate. I peeped in and saw my friend talking to Ravi's mother and cousin. I told the guard that I had to take Ravi's medicines inside. Luckily, my friend saw me and got me a visitor's pass. I was allowed inside. The doctor was talking to Ravi's mother and cousin. Ravi was now in the X-ray room.

The two guys who had dropped us to the hospital were continuously calling my friend. We had to meet them. We told Ravi's mother that we had some small work to do. We came out of the hospital and met those guys at the parking lot. They were demanding a sum of 8,000 rupees.

After paying the hospital bills, I had only 4,000 rupees and my friend had just 500 bucks.

The two guys asked us whether Ravi's parents had reached the hospital. I replied in the affirmative. Thanking them, I gave them 4,000 rupees and told them to leave. One guy told me that he wanted to see Ravi and took my visitor's pass. We were made to sit in their car as he left. The guy holding us back in the car told us to give him 6,000 rupees. He said that there was a lot of blood in the back seat of their car and they had to spend a lot of money to clean it. It was their personal car and not an ambulance. After fifteen minutes, the guy who had gone inside the hospital returned. He let me and my friend go. They left the hospital.

As we returned to the hospital, Ravi's mother and cousin were standing outside. As soon as they saw us, they started shouting at us in front of everybody.We were petrified and confused as to why they were all of a sudden so angry and shouting at us. Earlier, they had spoken to us softly and were listening to us, but now they seemed to have no patience even to listen to us. They told us to leave the hospital. They were shifting Ravi to another hospital. They said they would take care of Ravi. We had no clue what that guy had told Ravi's mother and cousin. We later came to know that the guy had taken money from Ravi's mother too.

My friend was recovering from a minor bike accident in which he had hurt his knee. During the car accident, he had been hurt at the same place. He was unable to walk properly. It was around 10.30 at night and the hospital people wouldn't allow more than two people to stay. As the doctor said that Ravi was safe, we thought of leaving for home. We decided to come back the following morning.

My friend's phone battery had died. We reached his place at around 11.30. His dad was extremely angry and started shouting at us as to what had we done to Ravi. We started explaining to him what had actually happened. His dad interrupted us with a thunderous roar, "Hey, what are you guys talking about? Ravi is dead!"

There was absolute silence. I dropped to the ground and started sobbing bitterly.

Ravi died due to severe internal bleeding. It was the first death I saw from such close quarters and it had so much impact on me. Ravi was a very good friend of mine, but now I had lost him forever. I could not see him or talk to him anymore. Death is an exceptionally fallacious thing. It sucks. We just cannot digest it. It is exceedingly hard to believe it actually happens for real.

We were five people in the car. Except Ravi, the others had negligible or no injuries. Even the driver of our car had only minor injuries. But Ravi was dead. How was that even possible? Either all of us should have been dead or at least have had fatal injuries. Why did Ravi alone die? The doctors had assured us that he was fine and that there was no harm for his life. Still he had died. Was it already written in his destiny or was it just an accident? Was it meant to be? Was it God's plan? Had Ravi's time come?

Till date, I don't understand the mystery behind his death. Why did death happen only to him and why were we safe and still alive? Whom do we blame for Ravi's death? Fate? The car? The car driver? Was it the accident? Was it the doctor or the hospital? Maybe death had a specific pattern, a design in which it works. I don't know for sure how it works, but it does feel devastating and awfully mysterious.

Ravi's death was an unforgettable one, an unforgivable one. His death made things ruthless. I remember crying for days. Till this day, I have never cried so much for anybody or anything in the whole world. Ravi was a genuinely good person. He had no enemies; everyone loved him. He never got angry and had a very good sense of humour. Even though he had many problems, he always hid them behind his honest smile. I am not telling all this because he is dead or to make you sentimental. That is the truth about him. He was a good generous person who stood by his friends at all times.

The photo in the introduction page was taken on the day of the accident. I never knew it would be the last day of his earthly life when we clicked that photo. There were a lot of clues about his impending death in the photos that we had clicked that day. I don't know whether it is just a coincidence, but in five or six photos there is clear evidence. Years later, he inspired me to write this book concerning death and raise questions about death.

They say that God takes back good people soon. But God, this isn't fair! You just can't do that. You shouldn't do that. You can't take the good people just like that. Ravi died on 29.09.2011. He was just 21 years old. We had celebrated his birthday three months ago. We never knew it would be his last birthday. I miss him. All his friends miss him, his parents and family too. Ravi, you will always be in our hearts and minds. This book is a small tribute to you.

Now that I look back at the accident, I wonder if the car that we were in had advanced braking technologies such as ABS (anti-lock braking system) and EBD (electronic braking device), would Ravi have survived the accident. The car was a basic, entry level sedan with no airbags. It was built for the Indian market concentrating more on 'mileage' than safety. Months after the accident, I learnt that the car had a faulty braking system at high speeds.

Can technology save lives? Well, technology may not stop death completely, but it can definitely reduce the number of accidents. Today, ABS and EBD are standards in almost all commercial cars, but it was not so back in 2011. ABS and EBD are saving thousands of lives every day by making travelling safer than ever before!

After a few days of the accident, someone posted a photo of our car on Facebook. The first comment on the post was, "All are spot-dead, uh?" The car was in such a bad shape that no one believed we came out alive. The four of us who survived were supposed to be dead that day. We are lucky to be alive till this day, but not RAVI!

Stage 29
The Change!

If you don't like something, then change it.
If you can't change it, then change your attitude.

- Maya Angelou

Change is rational, change is progress. Time changes, dates change, seasons change, winds change direction, jobs change, water changes into ice or vapour, iron changes into rust, the young change into the old, Mother Nature changes, engine oil is changed. Change is inevitable. The bus conductor gives change. Change is normal. Everything changes. Similarly, life changes into death. Even this book changed at several points of time, before it got this shape.

I guess we have talked enough. In fact, we have talked way too much about death. I know you will be kind of sad, reading all this and knowing all that. Everything is definitely going to end someday for sure. I can't lie to you sweetly to make you comfortable about death. Nobody or nothing has the power to alter, defy or escape death.

Death is going to come to us someday. It can even come all of a sudden. It takes just one heart attack. Boom, snap, you are gone. Who has even the slightest idea about death? But we still have a decent lifespan to do a lot, before time runs out.

Don't say you have no time. Everybody has got twenty-four hours in a day. Nobody has got a minute more than that. We only have one lifetime. We should do everything that we ever want to do, before the game is over. There is no one else in the world who can lead our life on our behalf.

A few people say life is meaningless. Some say life is a short journey. Others say life is not about finding yourself, but about creating yourself. For many, life is all about making money. Life is an adventure or a kind of sport for some. There are people who think life is a bitch. For some people, being happy is the only thing that matters. For a few, living their dreams is the definition of life. What is your definition of life?

I feel that life is a chance, a platform and an opportunity to do whatever we wish to do. Life is a book that consists of blank pages, nothing is written on it. It is up to every individual to fill the pages they want to. The filled pages are the past, we can only go through them, but we cannot erase them. Some pages make us happy, some pages make us sad, some pages make us regret for writing them. We may even want to tear down a couple of pages. The blank and unfilled pages are for the future; they are still empty. We decide what needs to be written. Do you want to write what you have always written? The book is half-empty!

We all have just one book, with a limited number of pages. A maximum of 36,525 pages! We never know which day is the last page of the book. We can spend it doing good or bad, we can live up to our dreams, follow our heart, go with the flow, make a lot of money, become successful, marry the one we love, celebrate life, complain about life, blame others for our lives turning out this way or do whatever else we want to. Life is all about the choices we make and the chances we take. Live life, don't just survive.

Are you alive or just breathing? The best way to live life is to make use of every day to its fullest potential. Use this opportunity to live a fulfilling life.

Life is a predestined one-way trip to death. Once we spend a day, that day is over. We are never going to get the same day again. The only thing that we cannot recycle is time. What did you do today? Were you happy with what you did today? Don't waste any part of today, because you will never get it again. Every day is today, tomorrow never comes.

So whom are you living your life for? Yourself or for other's sake? Do you bother about what other people think about you? Are you passionately following your dreams? Have you found your burning desire? What is your secret ingredient? Is this the life you always wanted to live? Are you happy with what you are getting? Who decides what and how your life is going to be? Do you love the job you are doing or are you just doing it because it is paying you pretty well and is giving security? Do you feel like quitting your job and finding a better job, a job that you love to do? Will you take risks? Are you are making yourself comfortable and compromising in every step, because you have a family to take care of, many commitments, promises to keep and your own stomach to feed? There are EMIs to be paid, loans to be cleared, expenses such as vehicle fuel and so on. In the process, we are giving up on our dreams and are focused on catching the things that life throws at us.

Don't ever compare your life with others. If you do so, then you are insulting yourself. Do you feel as though you and someone else are from the same hometown, went to the same school and engineering college, the other person is more successful? But does he have the same talent, strength, dream and passion you have? He may have worked hard or maybe he just got lucky. Some birds are just aren't meant to be caged. He didn't tread the same path as you did; you don't know what his journey is all about. So why compare your journey with his? It will only make you feel bad and that is not going to help you in any way.

We all have only one life. Then why are we compromising, adjusting and limiting ourselves? Why do we say certain things are out of reach and we cannot do them? Why do we live for others' sake? We have to be bold, confident and believe in ourselves and our dream. Don't say you can't do a task, because you can. How and where do you want to be in the next five years? And five years is really not a long time… it's just 1,825 days! You may have committed a lot of mistakes in the past, but you have to let go of them now. Learn from those mistakes, before they become regrets. Regretting sucks out the hope inside you. It doesn't make things any better. You still have time. Some time. Find what you want, live your life as you always wanted to. Don't go against your will, it will never keep you happy. What else on earth matters to you other than your own happiness?

This is your life. Do what you love and do it more often. If you don't like something, then change it. If you don't love your job, quit. If you don't have enough time, stop watching TV. If you are looking for the love of your life, stop. They will be waiting for you when you start doing the things you love. Start doing the things that you love. Stop over analysing – life is simple. All emotions are beautiful.

When you eat, appreciate every bite. Open your mind, arms and heart to new things and people. We all are united in our differences. Ask the person next to you what their passion is and share your inspiring dream with him or her. Travel more often, getting lost will help you find your trueself. Some opportunities come only once, seize them. Life is all about the people you meet and the things you create with them.

Humans always have a tendency to blame others and the external factors for their lives becoming 'like this.' What is the point in complaining and blaming others? It is not going to do any good to us or others. We need to stop blaming others or giving excuses and be responsible and fix the mess. No one else is going to do this for us. We are in no position to expect things from others. Don't expect any miracles to happen, because they have stopped showing up. It's time to create the miracles. God is not going to come down physically and solve our problems. Stop waiting for Him. He has TOO much to take care of. In order to be successful, we need to dream big, think, plan, take action, monitor the progress, take feedback, keep working, never quit, and create your way for a successful life. You can be successful, because most people out there are lazy.

Your life is not only yours, it is connected to so many other people around you: your parents, relatives, spouse, children, grandchildren, friends and so on. They all are an important aspect of your life. But do all those people really know who you are inside? What are your desires? What is running in that giant brain of yours? What do you want in your life? Who does your heart beat for? Where do you want to go? What is your destiny? Are people aware of the big dreams you are carrying? Who are you in love with, who do you want to get married to? (That's the same question, I suppose.) Some may know them, but not everyone. Don't compromise anything for anyone just because it makes them happy; it may screw your happiness forever.

Life is too short to wake up in the morning with regrets. So love the people who treat you right and forget the ones who don't. Believe that everything happens for a reason. If you get a chance, take it; if it changes your life, let it. Nobody promised that it is going to be easy. They just promised it would be worth doing it. Take chances, spend money on the things you love, laugh till your stomach hurts and dance as if no one is watching you. When you are in some problem, start singing; you will realise your voice is much worse than your problems. Have some sense of humour. Pose stupidly to photos, be childlike, think outside the circle, write a bucket list, stop planning and start doing. Don't wait to achieve perfection, you will never be perfect. Take more pictures, walk in the rain, eat good food, write letters and send greeting cards to faraway friends. Live life! If you don't do anything stupid while you are young, you won't have anything to laugh at old age. Life is extremely short to remove the USB safely.

Sometimes I wonder who on earth has everything? Who is that person who is completely satisfied and doesn't need anything more? Poor people don't have money, but they seem to be happy. The rich, in spite of loads of money, don't seem to be finding peace of mind in their lives. Some are worried how they would leave everything on earth and go back empty-handed. Not in all cases. Nope. Of course, everything cannot be either true or false for all the cases. They do differ.

What defines a happy life? Money, power, being a politician in India, social status, the number of WhatsApp groups you are the administrator of, the number of Facebook friends or Twitter followers you have, love, relationships, a long and healthy life, expensive cars, a chartered flight or a private 333 feet yacht? Happiness is an art. It is a journey and not a destination. Happiness begins not with your job, partner or money, but with YOU!

Being happy is a choice. Happiness is merely an internal affair, not an external one. We cannot own happiness; we can only pursue it. There is no Y in HappYness, there is only an I in HappIness. Happiness is a noun, not an adjective. Instead of being with someone who makes you happy, be that someone that makes you happy. It makes a lot of difference. We always seek happiness from others; we never understand that the true reason behind our happiness is our own selves. I love this Buddha's saying: "There is no path to happiness. Happiness is the path!"

No one likes Mondays, job, school, homework, fake friends, waiting, long queues, being ignored, rejection, drama, an empty fridge, being replaced, low battery and a slow internet. I wish life was a single straight highway with no tollbooths. Unfortunately, it isn't. There should be ups and downs in life. A---------------line in the ECG monitor symbolises death. There comes a certain time in life when we feel we haven't solved our problems yet. There will be times when everything seems to be going just right, as planned, a knife stabs at our back. Many things and people are far gone in life, just like that, in a flash, because we didn't care, we were too busy, we thought they would come back and we never even tried to stop them from going. Now they are long gone. Well, that doesn't mean that we are not happy or they are not happy. Everyone is happy, but NOT with the same person anymore.

I love Woody Allen's perspective of life: "Life is wrong; it should be backwards. We should die first, so we can get it over with. Then we live in a retirement house, until we are not too old enough to be there and we start getting paid our pension. Then we start working with a golden Rolex. We work for forty years, until we are pretty young to enjoy retirement. We go from party to party, drink, have sex, and then we start school and play with our friends, with no kind of responsibility, until we become a baby and the last nine months we are really comfortable in our mother's womb, all exclusive. At the end, we leave the world with an awesome orgasm." That's pretty orgasmic, right? How would life have been with this reality? Would it be more thrilling and fun than what it is now?

Some people are so rich in this planet that they don't even know what to do with so much money. Are they going to take it with them to heaven or hell, if they exist? No. They cannot take a single penny with them. Yeah, there may be some spare change in their pockets at the time of their death, but can they spend it on popcorn while watching *Bruce Almighty* in the gold class theatre of heaven? They may not take anything with them, but they leave behind many things: money, land, house, cars, assets, gold and so on. This ultimately belongs to their wife, kids and grandchildren, who will lead a luxurious life. Are these luxurious people going to live forever? One day even they will accompany their ancestors.

The earth consists of all the kinds of people. There are good, bad, rich, poor, hungry, starving, overweighed, intelligent and stupid people. There are people who want to save the world, others who want to destroy the planet. There are life savers, murderers, saints, sinners, serial killers, underworld dons, healthy and the sick. There are thousands who are just born, and another thousands are at the verge of dying. Some are dying, RIGHT NOW… as you are reading this word, this line. There are people who believe in God and heaven. There are people who believe that God doesn't even exist. There are people working for world peace and there are terrorists planning to destroy world peace and kill thousands of innocent men, women and children.

It is tough to live our lives by ourselves, leaving everything behind. It is hard to change for good and live the life that is destined for us. There may be a few insecurities. Some people who are close to us may not like all that we are planning to do. But they are your dreams goddamn it! You are the one who hears those tiny little voices in your head. Maybe you are hearing them, but are not listening to them. It may be 'difficult' to follow your dream, but it's a 'tragedy' not to! You have to fall in love with yourself, your dreams and your life. Don't worry about the money initially, do what you love, love what you do. Gradually, figure out how you can make a living out of something that you love so much, that you don't mind doing it for free. As Confucius said, "If you love your job, then you don't have to work even for a single day."

The rich are becoming richer, the poor are becoming poorer. People control people.There is a certain class of people who create the rules and laws and impose them to be followed by the other people. They decide who gets what. What price do we need to pay to get it? People pay taxes, but are unaware where all their money goes and who is benefitted. They create scarcity with an increase in demand, which increases the price.They call themselves the higher authority, and promise to clean up the mess they have created all by themselves, and work for the betterment of society, men, woman and children.They say they will make the world a better place to live in and they say they will do good to people, and claim that they are doing it. But are they?

Most of the times people do things that absolutely make no sense. They hate their jobs, but they still keep doing it. They say they'll quit, but they will never. People first spend their health gaining wealth and then spend all their wealth to regain their health. They love someone, but marry someone else. They are afraid to tell the truth. Yeah, the truth hurts; so people lie.

They say time heals and changes everything, but the truth is we need to change according to time. Success isn't a fortnight business. Success takes time, patience, self-belief, confidence, smart work, focus, dedication, persistence, purpose, consistency and, most importantly, a big dream to begin with. Hang in there, before giving up, give it another last try. Who knows what will happen when you try. It just has to work out once. Have patience; the seed that you sow today decides which fruit it bears in the future. The seed takes time to grow into a tree. Rome was not built in 3 days!

Success brings fame, fame brings money. But money brings nothing. It cannot buy happiness. Wait! What? Well, money can buy you a Jet Ski. I have never seen anyone sad on a Jet Ski. A saying goes: "Money may not buy you happiness, but it is comfortable to cry in a BMW than on a bicycle." Many of the people who say money cannot buy happiness are either poor or do not know where to shop for it. Oh poor, get rich! The lack of money is the root of all evil. It's good to have money and the things that money can buy. But it's good too, to checkup once in a while that you haven't lost the things that money can't buy!

You are not only the hero of your life, you are also the director. In life, when nothing goes right, go left. Trust and let it go. If it's meant to be yours, it will be yours. First know the rules, then you can **!3® €@!<** them. Don't use seven words, if four will do. It is always better to die on your feet than to live on your knees. There will be a few times when we do wonder if life is supposed to be like this. People don't believe in what you say; people only believe in what you do. You may not necessarily be perfect, but your success has to be perfect.

Success is a journey of ups and downs. It is not merely a destination. Do you remember the moral story taught to us in childhood? "Slow and steady wins the race." Life is all about forgetting what you were and focusing on what you want to be. Remember: Anything may kill you, anywhere, anytime!

The moral of the story is: Death is not the greatest loss in life, loss is when life dies inside you, when you are still alive. Celebrate the event called life. One day you will just be a memory to the other people; make sure you are a good memory. We are all here for a very limited period of time. Let's use the time wisely and concentrate on being happy. In order to make others happy, we need to be happy first. Help the poor and the needy; if we cannot help or don't want to help others, let us at least cause no harm or hurt others. Forgive others for everything, not because they deserve forgiveness but you deserve peace. Nothing is worthy if you are not happy.

There are various kinds of people, categorised into continents, countries, religion, race, gender, tradition, culture, language spoken, the God they believe in and so on. Everybody claims that they are unique, their perspective is different and they are better than most of the other people alive. Yes, every single person is unique. But if we carefully watch them, dig a little deep, all the people on earth are almost the same. Of course, we all are Homo sapiens.

Everyone needs happiness, success, money, faithful friends, a peaceful mind, a happy relationship, good health, a beautiful girlfriend, a rich and handsome boyfriend, big dream, fame, a luxurious life and a loving spouse. Everyone wants to party, make more money, go on long drives, have a nice and peaceful sleep, enjoy, do the crazy stuff, eat tasty and healthy food, marry the one they love, have kids, get a good job, make more money, go on a vacation, spend time for themselves, see the happiness in their parents' eyes by they being the reason and do a million other things. How different are we from each other in the big picture?

Every day, make at least two people happy. Make sure one of them is you. You may lead all your life telling lies to others, but be true to yourself. Find the right purpose in life and live up to it. I know saying all this is easy, living up to all this is very tough. Even I am struggling to break out of this cage. I found one of my life's purposes. It took me many years, a lot of failures, millions of mistakes, bad decisions and wrong steps before getting here. Here I am today a writer.

We have brains in our head and feet in our shoes. We can literally steer ourselves to any corner of the world. The only limits are our thoughts, self-limiting beliefs and small dreams. Always dream big; it takes the same amount of time and energy to dream a big dream and a small dream. If you don't like it here, then move on. Remember that you are not a tree.

The heart follows where the head goes. The heart tells us where to go and the brain tells us how to go. Don't be sorry for yesterday, be thankful for today. Seriousness takes time, a pretty long time. It is just difficult, not impossible. Go behind your dreams. If you find risk, take it, bite it, grind it, taste it, eat it, ingest it, digest it and make it your shit. Life is too short to regret the past. How much guilty can a man be?

According to me, there are only three kinds of people in the world: the one who never tries, the one who tries but quits and the one who never quits trying. Which category do you fall into? Life is all about the choices you make, the big dreams you carry and the things that you do. Your decision defines your destiny. Everything you ever need is on the other side of fear. Taking action is an important part of success. Believe it is possible, because it is. You have to believe in yourselves, when no one else does. If you fail to believe in yourself, then who else will?

Life isn't fair, but it is still good. If you don't go behind what you want, then you will never get it. If you are not daring enough to ask, then the answer will always be 'no.' If you don't fight for what you want, then don't cry for what you have lost. If you do not step forward, you will always remain in the same place. Whenever you think of giving up, think of all the people that would love to see you fail. It doesn't matter how many opportunities you have, if you don't know how to utilise them. Dream and live as if it is impossible to fail. If it takes two minutes to do it, then do it immediately. I am not talking about making Maggi noodles here.

The world is very complex. Half of the world consists of people who are extra-ordinarily rich, own expensive cars, chartered flights, bungalows, private yachts, hundreds of businesses, casinos, black money and so on. The other of the world hardly has food to eat even once a day. There is nobody to take care of them, they are sick, they don't have a roof over their head, they sleep on the streets and they beg for food.

People are literally starving to death on one hand and on the other hand people are throwing good food in the garbage, just because they thought they could eat everything they saw at the buffet table. The food looked nice, but it didn't excite their senses. Now the food is going straight into the dustbin. Tonnes and tonnes of food is being wasted every day, while many people do not even have a handful of food. Before serving yourself, ask yourself if you are really going to eat everything that you are loading on your plate.

Well, if you really need more food, you can always take a second helping. There is nothing wrong in doing that. But who cares for all this? Everybody is worried only about their stomach, including me. If I am full, that's enough. That's all that matters. Are we not supposed to think about the starving people in the world? They too have a life, just like us, and are a part of the planet earth and the children of Mother Nature. Even if we don't feed the hungry, let us take a pledge to respect food and stop wasting it. Nobody is going to hang you for wasting food, but does that mean you should?

We have plenty of clothes, so many that we are often confused which one to wear to the weekend party. But one part of the world is lying naked. We always tend to complain about office air-conditioning, while some people don't even have enough fresh air to breathe. We get pissed off when someone accidently turns off the Wi-Fi; we don't care about poverty starving people to death. Realise the reality with your real eyes. It's never too late to start. Real happiness is felt and found when we see happiness in others' eyes due to us. And in the end, how much worse can it get? "People need everything permanent for a temporary life!"

When we are young, we have the time and energy, but no money. When we are adults, we have money and energy, but no time. When we are at old age, we have money and time, but no energy. Take some time today to experience the delight life brings, take some time to capture all the beautiful moments, take some time today to relieve all your glorious achievements. Take some time today, before time slips away forever.

It doesn't really matter who we are, where we are from and what we did. It all comes to an end someday, sooner or later. Some are kilometres away from death, while others are only a few inches away. So what is the point in living a life hating someone, being jealous, afraid of the society, scared of enemies, having grudges and not talking to certain people and taking revenge? In the long run, what are you going to get by taking revenge? Will you derive satisfaction? Really? There are lots of better stuff to do and get satisfaction from. There is only one bristle life, who knows what will happen when? And all we are busy doing is SHIT?

Life comes with an expiry date. But unlike medicines and organic products, the expiry date isn't printed on it. Life could expire anytime, anywhere and in any way. So make the most of it when it's still on. Stay on the track, believe in yourselves and your dreams. Don't let that inner voice fade away. If you are too worried about what other people think about you, then you become their slaves. Opinions are like assholes, everybody has one and it stinks.

If you are dependent, then you will be dominated. Some people are nicely gift-wrapped boxes of shit. Don't listen to them, they pretend that they care, but they don't. They let you down and insult you. They shout and scream at you that you cannot do it, they remind you of the past that you have forgotten, they will show you your limits, create boundaries and call you mad. They are assholes. All that comes out of them is shit; even if they are quiet, they still stink. They are dream-stealers. They don't do anything great in their lives and won't let others reach their destiny. They are busy letting people down, discouraging them and making others feel bad about themselves.

Don't listen to everyone around you. You follow your path and become successful. Then one day on the journey of life, you will definitely come across them. Talk to them then. Forget that they even exist now. As Bill Gates said, "If you are born poor it is not your mistake, but if you die poor then definitely it is your mistake."

It is not the miracles that changed the world. Great people were once ordinary people, just like you and me. History talks of men and woman who rose against all odds, broke the rules, never gave up and succeeded in their respective fields, resulting in the creation of a better world. Today we create history in our browsers every day and delete them before going to bed.

The one and the only person who is going to be with you all the time, right from your birth, childhood, school, adulthood, college, graduation, job, after marriage, old age and ultimately when you take your that last breath and finally die is "**YOU!**" Not your parents, spouse, relatives or friends. They will be present in your lives, but for how long? You alone have to run your life's marathon. Others can guide, help and accompany you, but you have to run on your own. You can bring the horse near the pond, but you cannot make it drink the water. They can give you the roadmap, but you have to drive!

We spend most of the time with ourselves. No one else can lead our lives. We have to walk all the way alone. Others may come and go, advise you, seek your help, give you money, scold you, and try to tell you what is good and bad or right and wrong. They may even sleep with you. But in the long run, we have to do it on our own. Self-service is the best service. You can't hire someone to do push-ups for you. People will come into your life and go. That is not the end of the story, it is the end of their part in the story.

The following lines are very powerful, inspiring, simple and motivational. I want to share them with you.

"If you have food in your fridge, clothes on your back, a roof over your head and a place to sleep, then you are richer than 50 per cent of the world."

"If you have money in the bank, your wallet and some spare change, you are among 8% of the world's wealthy."

"If you woke up this morning with more health than illness, you are blessed than the millions of people who will not survive by this week."

"If you can read this, you are more fortunate than 2.5 billion people who cannot read at all."

- Anonyms

Theoretically, nothing should stop or slow you down from creating the life of your dreams, other than the terrific traffic jams on those busy crowded streets. We always forget that we have the power to change things and change the world. We wait for other people and God to work miracles for us.

Miracles don't just happen. This is the 21st century. All the gods who once visited earth have gone back. They may or may not return, but they are not going to show up anytime soon and do any miracle for us. We have the power and capacity to perform miracles. Life becomes so much easier when we stop being nice to stupid people. You have to try all the possibilities before giving up. You never know which key unlocks which door. There is no problem without a possible solution. They manufacture the locks, along with the keys. We all have the locks; we just have to find the right key and unlock the doors.

Do not let the fear of failure stop you from doing things. Failure is an important part of success. Failure teaches us to do the same thing again, only wiser and better than the previous time. How will you even know whether it's a good or bad decision if you don't make it? If people are talking behind your back, remember you are already one step ahead of them. No one else can live your life and get you out your mess. You alone are the reason and the result of what you are today. You can either choose to remain a victim by blaming others or take 100 per cent responsibility of your life. Remember you are the CEO of your life.

Our mind always either rattles in the past or worries about the future so much that we forget to live, feel and experience 'the present moment.' This moment is your life.

Live in the present moment. Don't indulge your mind in unwanted thoughts. Instead focus 100 per cent on what you are doing. When you are eating, just eat; when you are walking, just walk. Relax, take a deep breath and observe what is happening around you. Don't just live. Stay alive every passing moment. Not a single moment comes back. The past is long gone and the future is yet to come. It's what you do today that defines all your tomorrow. You reap what you sow. There is always more to life than sleeping, shitting, working, partying and watching TV. Always stay positive. Savour the delight of every passing moment to its fullest.

Don't wait for anyone to come and fix your problems, because honestly no one is going to come. Success is a choice, not an accident. What is your worth on earth? Time heals everything; give it time, some time. Get up and get to work. You have a thousand years to take rest and sleep once you are dead. Your life will change forever when you stop sleeping and start living.

There is always a second chance, but not for the same mistake. Always try to do new mistakes; there are billions of new mistakes to do. Only then you get the experience to do the things right. Take it or leave it. You are going to be old someday; do not regret not having tried. You are going to die someday. So do what you want to do and then die. There is no lock without a key. You have to find the key that opens the door to success, happiness and a better life. You deserve it all. Do not worry about buying a Lamborghini, worry about how you are going to drive it on the bad Indian roads.

Don't cry for what you lost yesterday, it was never really yours. You didn't bring anything along when you were born, remember? What is yours today is going to be someone else's tomorrow. You can't even take anything with you once you are dead. We are not here to own anything or to take anything. We are only here to utilise things, make the good use of them and make this one-time offer of life worthwhile. Today, the world has become so ironic. Instead of loving people and using things, we are loving things and using people.

Before your grave is filled with the tears of your loved ones, go do something good for them. Instead of sending flowers after someone is dead, do it when they are alive. Your blood is still flowing; you are still breathing. Your heart is still beating, babe and you are still alive, dude! That's the only reason! "We ain't dead yet." There is always hope. Life is a lesson, learn it. In the end, there is only one winner – YOU. You can do it. All you need is to believe.

Get busy living or get busy dying!

Stage 30
Why does Life Exist Only on Earth?

I shall never believe that God plays the dice with the universe.

- Albert Einstein

The earth is the only known planet in the entire universe that can sustain life. The universe is 13.7 billion years old and our earth is 4.55 billion years old and the existence of life is traced back to 3.3 billion years. The earth began its journey as a gigantic ball filled with numerous hot gases, which over time cooled down forming the core, crust, land, mountains, oceans, atmosphere, environment, nature, clouds and oxygen, resulting in the formation of life gradually.

Out of the billions of other galaxies, planets and trillions of stars, why was life put on earth alone? Was it an accident or a just a coincidence? Was earth perfectly placed in the third position from the sun at a distance of 150 million kilometres, resulting in conditions that were neither too hot nor too cold to sustain life's existence? Mercury and Venus are way too hot. Mars, Jupiter and other gas giants are extremely cold to sustain life. So far, the earth is the only known planet with water, breathable oxygen and perfect gravitational force to live in.

Science says the Big Bang caused earth and life. Religion says God is the creator of earth and the life in it.

Did God cause the Big Bang? Science has revealed more mysterious things about our universe in the past 300 years than religion has done in the past 10,000 years. What about the aliens? If they do exist, then who created them? God or the Big Bang? What do aliens believe their origin to be? Do they even know about God? Have they found God? Humans also haven't found Him yet, but we do believe that He exists somewhere out there, very far away, watching our every move!

If there is creation, then there is a creator. If God is the creator of earth, then which God created it? There are so many gods that we know. The three major religious groups of the world, Christianity, Islam and Hinduism, declare their God is the hero behind creation. But which God is it exactly? If all the three gods created earth, then shouldn't there be three earths? Unfortunately, there is just one. Did the gods divide the massive project of creation among themselves saying the Christian god would create America, Canada and Japan, the Hindu god would take over Asia and the Muslim god would create Europe, West Asia and the rest of the world?

May be all the gods had very good understanding among each other that they decided to create the human form in an identical manner, with the same specifications of the brain, heart, lungs, kidneys, liver, nervous system, spinal cord, muscles, intestine, digestive system, reproductive system, bones, blood, DNA, genes, tissues, cells, hair, skin, eyes and ears. Human beings on earth are fighting in the name of religion, whereas the gods above seem to be very cool with each other's perspectives.

How does the 'multiple gods' creation' theory explain the beginning of life?

Did the three gods come from three different directions for a common cause, which resulted in the Big Bang and later led to the formation of the earth? Once the earth was capable of sustaining life with sunlight, moon, land, water, oxygen, mountains, trees, plants and animals, did the three gods make their 'prototype' according to their own religion? Were these prototypes placed in three different parts of the world? Were these male and female prototypes allowed to freely use all the resources on earth? Could they eat whatever they wanted and roam wherever they wanted to? Their job then was to worship God, mate, reproduce, multiply and build their generation with the respective religious beliefs and spread them across the planet.

Did it then continue like this? The kids the male and female bore in the process would belong to the religion of their parents. Thus started humanity millions of years ago and generations and generations were born. They lived, died and also went back to their own respective gods, right back to where they came from. We are here today in the year 2016 of the 21st century believing and following the rules laid down by religion and we ask no questions.

People have been following the same rules for generations and we are going to teach the same rules to our future generation. We are going to tell them that they belong to a particular religion and that no further questions would be entertained. Kids grow up with what they have been taught right from the beginning. They are going to follow the same for the rest of their lives. Even though some have questions and doubts, their voices will slowly be silenced, either by choice or by force.

Spirituality and religion are entirely two different things. Spirituality unites people whereas religion divides people. We all are united by God and divided by religion. Morality is doing what is right, regardless of what you are told. Religion is doing what you are told, regardless of what is right. How ironic can this get? In the modern world, religion is one of the major categories in which people are divided.

Take for instance what happened in our country. In India, until the year 1947, there was absolutely no problem between any of the religious groups, especially the Hindus and Muslims, even though they were ruled by the Christian natives. What went so terribly wrong when the British finally decided to give us independence? All of a sudden there was an argument for two separate countries for two different religions. Where did this argument even come from? How did it all begin? We were living so peacefully for centuries together and out of nowhere we wanted two separate nations in the name of religion. There were raging fights, communal disputes, attacks, robberies and protests once India and Pakistan were partitioned. The worst thing was the British kept the separation boundary line between India and Pakistan a secret till the independence of both of the countries.

People in those times and historians today believe that if the British had revealed the borders before the independence and given some time to the people to choose sides, it wouldn't have triggered so much violence. Millions of people belonging to India were in the Pakistan side and Pakistanis were trapped on Indian soil. In the process of this transfer from one country to another, millions of people lost their houses, jobs, friends, farms and lands on which they were living for generations.

The shifting process led to starvation, lack of water and medical aid and sanitary problems. Some rich people had bullock carts, which made their journeys easier, while eighty to ninety per cent of the poor people had to walk all the way for around 150 kilometres across the border. In that hot weather, with no proper food or water and attacks every now and then, people dropped their belongings on the way as they were very tired walking for days together. Many people died in their journey of starvation, sun stroke and religious attacks.

Even the fight for freedom had not cause so many deaths as the partition did. There was total chaos. People were scared, helpless and unaware of what was going to happen to them. There were attempts made for a united India, but it failed in the last few meetings and all the leaders made a decision to partition the country into two. After independence, three wars have been fought between India and Pakistan. Today, India and Pakistan are rival nations. Many Indians hate Pakistan and everything that they stand for; and many in Pakistan hate us. Why? We don't know, we don't even need a reason, we just hate each other. In fact, a cricket match between India and Pakistan is not just a game; it is a kind of war in itself. Who is to be blamed? Religion or political leaders? Either ways, the consequences are suffered by the innocent people; they always pay the price. Who was happy and who benefitted from this separation? India, Pakistan, both or NONE?

The political leaders back then had planned to stay united and friendly, after the separation of the two countries. It is like getting a divorce and then getting married. Unfortunately, till date it has never happened, despite numerous attempts. All attempts have only failed.

In the modern world, people are fighting, making money and even dying in the name of religion. In the name of religion, huge wealth is amassed. All religious places have huge donation boxes. We have to pray, drop money in the box and then our work is done apparently. People beg on the streets in the name of God, showing idols and photos. Our education system is also not spared. There is religion and caste-based categories and reservations in schools and colleges. There is something called the caste certificate. There are people who even fake their caste on paper, to enjoy more benefits and reservation. When it comes to marriage too, religion and caste are priorities.

What if there was one single religion across the world? Would the world be a much better place to live in? I don't know how many people are actually benefitted by caste and religion. But religion has caused a lot of trouble, fight, rage, violence, chaos and death.

Every religion has its own God, faith, beliefs, preaching, philosophies, traditions, cultures, place of worship, style of praying, spiritual scriptures, prayer houses, festivals, offerings, sacrifices, attractions, policies, terms, conditions and dos and don'ts. Each religion claims that it is right, perfect, awesome and better than the other religion. Everyone tends to think that their shit smells SWEETER than the others'. If you question the ethics of religion, then be prepared for attacks, fights, protests, controversies, legal issues, bans and even war.

Religion is designed in such a way that a Christian is expected to pray only to the Christian God. He is a true Christian and only the Christian God can solve his problem, answer his questions, give him whatever he needs and fulfil his wishes. A Christian cannot make an emergency call to a Hindu or Muslim god. Will the God deny access to his calls? Would He say, "Try praying to your own god. I can't and I won't help you, because you do not belong to my religion. I am extremely sorry but you have dialled the wrong department"? How does it even work? Will this be treated as a crime? Do the prayers of different religions have different frequencies, channels and bandwidths?

Let's say a Hindu is in need of blood and he goes to the blood bank. Does he ask for two pints of B+ Hindu blood? Is there any difference between the blood of people from different religions? How can the different gods be capable of creating the exact same recipe for blood? Gods above may be fine with any religion, but the humans down here are not. We humans are ready to shed blood for the sake of religion.

What have we done? Won't a Christian's kidney fit into a Muslim's body? Won't a Muslim's eye make the Hindu see? Won't a Hindu's blood flow in a Christian's body? What is the difference between all of us? How can religion be defined? Just based on the parents we are born to? Are we a Christian if we are born in a Christian family? If our parents are Muslims, then are we Muslims too? What if they were Hindus? Then are we Hindus too? As Aamir Khan asks in the movie *PK*, *"Ye bhagwan 'tappa' kidar lagaatha hai bhai?* (where does God stamp the trademark of religion, bro?)"

People die fighting for the sake of protecting their religion and God. He has created all of us, everything that we see, hear and feel around us. How can we protect God residing in this tiny planet in such an enormous universe? God can protect us. How can we protect him by fighting with other religions? Ridiculous!

Buddhism was founded by Gautama Buddha, Jainism by Vardhaman Mahavira, Sikhism by Guru Nanak and Taoism by Laozi. They were ordinary people just like any of us before they encountered spirituality and self-realisation. They then found the true meaning and purpose of life and set out in quest of answers and complete knowledge. Once they were enlightened, they found their own ideologies. People who found their words, teachings and preaching meaningful and worth living for joined them or got converted to that particular religion. Did God create religion? Okay, I get you. Did the gods create religion? Or did man create it?

So what is the truth? We only know what others have told us to be the truth. But is that the truth? How do they even know that this is the truth? Did God tell them? Have they seen God? People for generations have believed something to be the truth because their ancestors told them so. Is that really the truth? Humanity's existence is traced back to tens and thousands of years. How many times has the truth been altered, modified, changed, improvised, destroyed and forgotten? How many new truths have been created? What is the future of all this truth? The future of this truth will be what we are going to tell to our future generations. But what is the truth? Do we even know the truth to tell them the truth?

This is ridiculously and mysteriously complicated. So did God create the earth and the life on it? Let's not worry about which god created all this, rather let us wonder and focus on why He did create it. Why did God even create earth, life and the human beings? What on earth are we here for? Did God feel bored being all alone that He created the planet and the human beings?

Why did God wait for so many years to create us? What was He doing before He created all this? Was He just travelling from one galaxy to the other, searching for a right place to set up a world that was suitable to sustain life? In His quest, did He stumble upon the Milky Way galaxy and the earth? Did He use all His creative ideas to create the world that we see, hear, feel, sense and pursue today? Are we all alone in the entire universe or is it that earth is just another branch office of God?

Did God create us just because He desperately needed some followers, believers, and worshippers who would praise Him, pray to Him and beg Him for favours? In return for favours, we give Him money (in the form of offerings), do sacrifices, *puja*, fast, sacrificing non-veg for two times a week, burn candles, light lamps and blast bombs to kill thousands of innocent people in the name of religion – so that He will give us what we want. Is He expecting us to do all these dramas for a return favour?

Many people pray to God to reap some kind of benefit. It may be more money, better health, peace of mind, someone is sick, for savoring the bliss of heaven, or whatsoever. And in return they offer *pujas*, sacrifices, offerings and so on. How many of us humbly pray with no demands and expecting nothing in return from God? Is this devotion?

Isn't it selfish only to pray for a return favour from God? Suppose, if we knew that God wouldn't give us anything, how many of us would still pray to God?

Humans will never let the God be alone. We never give Him solitude time and personal space. Do we even allow Him to take rest, sleep or at least take a power nap? Prayers happen round-the-clock, non-stop. Some prayers start even before sunrise, some happen all day long and a few are done all through the night. Yeah, it is all the matter of faith, but does He really give us everything that we ask for or does He choose whom to bless and which favours to fulfil? We all pray, but is He really listening? Is He enjoying our sacrifices? Do we need to please Him every single day in order to get things done? Will He take care of our needs only if we pray, praise, worship and perform sacrifices? If we do not pray, will He not consider our needs? Is that how it works?

Are all our prayers and sacrifices being delivered successfully to Him? There aren't any delivery reports or double blue ticks that confirm that our prayer has been delivered and He has read our prayers. Does God have enough time to listen and analyse all our prayer requests? Is He really enjoying all our prayers or is He just bored, sick and tired of all this?

Does He really expect us to do all this? Doesn't God know what we want, even if we don't ask Him for it? He's God for God's sake. He knows every goddamn thing. Why do we always make deals with God? You do this for me and in return I will do this for you. During our prayers, we always end up telling Him our woes and sharing our problems.

Who knows, God may be having problems of his own. Have we ever given a break to God and asked him, "God! How are you? Is everything fine? How is your job going on – looking after the earth and us? Is there something that I can do to help? How is the weather out there? Day by day, it's getting hotter and hotter in here!" He may be happy to listen to someone who is worried and concerned about Him.

God is literally present out there somewhere, right? What is He doing right now, what does He do every day and on weekends? Is He constantly monitoring our every move and each word that comes out of our mouth and our actions? Is He watching you as you're reading this book? There are 7.3 billion living people on this planet. Is He watching everyone at the same time? Apart from us, He also has to look after the animals, birds, insects, reptiles, fishes, plants, trees, rivers and everything else.

He also needs to take care of the sunlight reaching us, the breeze blowing on earth, and the amount of rainfall the earth receives, He has to maintain harmony and balance in nature; He has to foresee the earthquakes, floods, famine, and every single thing on earth. He also needs to keep his eyes on the dead – to judge and decide who goes where, heaven or hell. He has to watch over every aspect of life. So the constant piling of prayer requests every second can only add to his stress. Mercy be in his alley. Just imagine the kind of stress God would have, working constantly, with no sleep or breaks and way too much work. How many employees does He have to help him? Sounds like it is pretty tough to be God!

Apart from us, God has created numerous varieties of animals, birds, insects, reptiles, mammals, fishes and micro-organisms. What are they doing on earth? They have no clue about who God is and they do not worship Him.There are animals which are a threat to human beings and kill humans; there are animals which human beings prey on and eat them as his food. Whatever the God's plan was, today our planet is well-balanced with more than thirteen million known living species. There may be many other species that human beings haven't even discovered yet.

When man was first placed on earth, he was happy and surprised to see this beautifully engineered majestic creation of God that consisted of high mountains, millions of square miles of blue oceans, waterfalls, rivers, gigantic trees, a wide variety of plants, greenery, peaceful hill stations, tasty animals and all the other wonderful creations of God. But as human beings developed from cavemen, wanderers and food gatherers, he began to settle down in a place. He started agriculture, built homes, invented fire, began to cook and eat his food, became civilised and invented the wheel, which made transportation much easier. Gradually, he invented many more things that made his day-to-day life easier.

Today we live in the world where man has set foot on the moon, sent rovers to planet Mars, built the International Space Station that orbits the earth sixteen times a day at a speed of 27,000 kilometres an hour and built skyscrapers that are 163 floors tall, a kilometre from the land, touching the clouds. We have reached the top of Mount Everest and touched the floors of the ocean.

What do we not have on earth today? Electricity, computers, programming, internet, battery, smartphone, apps, cameras, printers, video games, TV, air-conditioner, refrigerator, washing machine, robots, musical instruments, watches, magnet, electromagnetic waves, iron, steel, engine, bike, car, bus, train, ship, submarine, aeroplane, jet, rocket, gun, bomb, missile, nuclear weapons, medicine, drugs, credit cards, condoms and millions of other inventions that have changed the way we live. We have come to a state where we cannot live without these. With today's technology, nothing seems impossible. We have broken all barriers and have created a world in which every single impossible thing is possible.

While creating the earth and human life, I don't think even God would have predicted that the earth would one day be so technologically advanced and human beings would be capable of doing so many things that God himself never did. God has created things but He hasn't invented anything. Man has invented many things with no help from God. In a way, we have surprised God, the creator himself.

But in the process, Mother Nature has been destroyed and exploited a lot. In the battle of survival of the fittest, millions of people starve to death, don't have fresh water to drink, proper clothes to wear, a roof over their head, and a bed to sleep on. Millions are unemployed and millions are begging and sleeping on the streets. What have we done to the world in the name of civilisation, development and advancement?

We are born on this planet, we learn to crawl, walk, run, go to school, study, graduate, fall in love, find a job, make money, become strong, get married, have kids and work almost all our lives. Our kids then grow up and get married, while we get old and finally die. We go through all these stages if we manage to stay alive, not commit suicide, are not killed by anyone, no disease or calamity harms us and we do not meet with any accident.

So why did God give us 36,525 days? Just to worship Him? To enjoy the beauty of nature and His creation? To explore and admire God's design of earth? To go to office and work in jobs we don't like? To make money? To buy expensive cars? To drink and party on weekends? To flirt with beautiful women? To get married, have sex, have children and then build a generation? To strive for the betterment of the planet? To feed the hungry? To help the needy? To work for world peace? To have a big dream and work for its fulfilment? Or is it that God wants us to find Him from where is He hiding? What does He want us to do with our lives? No matter what you choose to do or not do, in the end everything will come to an end. They say God created the universe from nothing. Is God + Nothing = Universe and Us? If God created everything, then who created God?

Stage 31
What is the Purpose of Life?

The two most important days in your life
are the day you are born,
And the day you find out why?

- Mark Twain

Life has existed on earth for millions of years now. Human existence dates back to several thousands of years. There are many similarities, characteristics and reasons to believe that humans were the originally evolved and are advanced versions of the ape family with a highly developed brain and reasoning power. Many believe all life forms on earth are created by God and He controls everything. But why is there life form only on earth and not on any other planet? Why did He choose only the earth? What is so special about it? Does life exist anywhere else other than the earth? What is the purpose behind the existence of life on earth?

Billions of people are born on this planet and billions are dead. About ninety-five per cent of the people who have lived on earth are now dead. Can earth be considered a big graveyard as there are more dead people than of living? We humans have evolved from hunters, wanderers and food gatherers to a settled and civilised society. Humans practiced agriculture and invented tools that made his daily life easy. He built houses to protect himself from animals, rains and natural calamities. He began to live in groups and started a family. Our ancestors never predicted the world would to become so technologically advanced. We human beings have achieved several things that seemed impossible 100 years ago. In the modern world, there is so much development in every field.

But what is the purpose of life? Why are we here on earth? What are our duties and responsibilities? Who is going to brief us of our real purpose? Is it destiny and fate? Or is life a set of blank pages that are to be written by us? Is there really any purpose to life? Does life have any meaning of its own?

If there is a purpose to life, then what is it? Is life all about experiencing each and every passing moment? Is it all about making money? Is it about staying happy? Is it living a good life? Is it getting settled? Is it being religious? Is it about worshipping and believing in God so that He will take us to heaven after we die? Is it about living for others? Is it about following our dreams? Is it about working for the good of the community or world peace? Is it about solving the problems of hunger, poverty and pollution? Is it all about making the planet a better place to live in? Is it all about living the way I want to, thinking about me and myself only as it is my life, since I am the captain of my own ship and I choose where to steer my ship should be none of others business?

Finding the true purpose of life can be very confusing sometimes. At times, we don't understand whether to still trust, believe and hold on or just let go. It is hard to wait for the right purpose, especially when the wrong purposes are so beautiful. There are always two wolves inside us. One urges us to do it and the other says don't do it. One says believe in it, trust in it, the other says don't even dare. One says we can do it and we will succeed and the other wolf asks what if we fail. Are we ready to face that embarrassment? Will we have the capacity to rise again? Well, which wolf will win at last? That's right. The one we feed and listen to will win.

Life is a journey; we all travel in a different space and time. Life without a purpose is like a journey without a destination. Though scientifically there is no specific purpose for life, over the years, people have found various purposes for their lives. For most of the people, money, fame and success matter the most. Other people live by their dreams and passion and aren't worried about money. The world is also filled with bad people: murderers, serial killers, rapists, thieves and terrorists.

There are people in love, those with broken hearts, cheats, those who have been betrayed and people with deadly diseases. Many people don't have food to eat, proper clothes to wear, clean water to drink and fresh air to breathe. There are people who live their entire lives for the betterment of others. They are not worried about their own needs. There are soldiers who serve the country, sacrificing their lives for the countrymen they don't even know.

There are people who are searching for life in another planet that can sustain living conditions. And there are people who don't even know what to do with their lives. They live, roam, eat and sleep on the streets. Some live only to eat and others only to drink. More than four billion people don't even have a purpose or reason to live – they are living just because they are not dead yet. There are people who lose all hope and commit suicide and there are people who want to live forever, make money, stay happy and celebrate the event called life.

People waste years of their lifetime without even knowing what to do. They take up a job and do it even if they don't like it, they sacrifice all their dreams to build a family, they save money for twenty to twenty-five years for their children's wedding and ultimately get their children married to the ones they choose and not the ones whom their children love. The children on the other hand don't want to hurt their parents and they agree to everything. In India, we have the freedom to choose our prime minister, but not our life partners. How ironic is that? But what people forget is this: we only have one life. Then why sacrifice and compromise? India may change one day, but Indians will never! Who even taught us to think and live like this? Why have we become like this? Is there an end to all this?

Who is crazy? Are we crazy or are they crazy? Who is right and who is wrong? Who is to be blamed for all this? Is there somebody really out there who is responsible and controlling all that this going on here? Are they watching our every move? Will they save us? Do all the good people really go to heaven? Well, who decides who is good and who is bad? No one is born evil, even the devil is a fallen angel.

Sometimes I feel that no one is bad and wrong at all. People do everything for a particular reason. The reason may be their own personal good, money, wealth, property, comfort, luxury or some other benefits. It may be for the happiness of their families and for the community's good. We may not be getting any benefits out of their actions. Considering this, can we call some people selfish and bad?

Well, who is not selfish? Don't we all think of our own good first? At the end of the day, everyone is bothered about their own stomach, solving the problems of their own and wishing for a better life than yesterday and a comforting sleep. Then they have a family to take care of and worry about. Don't judge someone because they sin differently than you.

Some people are happy working for others. Some are doing a job they don't even like, just because it has a steady cash flow and promises security. Some do not want to work for others, they want to start something on their own, but they don't have the money. How many people actually love their job and what they are doing? Why has the world turned out like this? Today nothing else matters: it's all about the money, everything is a business. At every instance in our life, somebody will be making money from us.

Sometimes, it becomes hard to understand whether we are wrong or the world is right. What if you are right and people tend to change you? What if everybody lies to you all the time? What if all you saw, heard, felt, said, experienced and made to believe was a well-planned and executed lie? What if everything was a myth, nothing really existed and we all were in somebody's dream? And then we wake up the next day only to realise it was just a dream all these days. What if the earth is a reality TV show for aliens and other intelligent life forms on the other planets?

In the final run, how did we live life? Did we live it for a purpose and for the right purpose? If there is a life, then definitely there is a purpose too. Life doesn't exist just like that. Even a clock that has stopped working shows the right time two times a day.

We are still humans. If you have already found a purpose to live with, good for you. You made it! If you have not found the purpose yet, keep looking. It may be right behind you, but you are not turning back to find it. Purposes are possible. Don't wait for thirty years to realize that you chose the wrong career and sixty years to realize that you married the wrong person and that you could have married the one you loved. Do not take ninety years old to find out the purpose of your life and realize that you could have lived and achieved your dream life. Start today, start somewhere. Follow your heart and dreams, money will come. And one day, life has to come to an end, as promised.

Stage 32
The Beginning

Each day is a little life, every waking and raising a little birth, every fresh morning a little youth, every going to rest and sleep is a little death.

- Arthur Schopenhauer

Our life begins with love. The husband and wife are united in marriage and start a life together. They make love to each other. We are the result of our parent's devotion. Out of the 250 million sperms, we outraged, defeated and won and made it to our mother's womb. The fight for survival begins long before we are born. Stage by stage, we take shape inside the womb for typically 266 days. Once the foetus is sufficiently developed, a chemical kicks off the process of birth, which begins with the foetus being pushed out of the birthing canal and we are born.

Happy birthday! It is birthday number zero. It is our first day on earth, the only planet that is suitable to sustain life. We are at the right place, at the right time and we have been successfully delivered. Our clock has just started ticking. We have a maximum of 36,525 days to live, love and explore.

We open our eyes to face the big world. We don't even know who we are. Where we are? Where have we come from? Why are we here? Why are we put in this world?

Who are our parents? We don't even know whether we are male or female. Which religion do we belong to and who is our God? It is apparently the only day in our life when we are crying and our mother is smiling happily. When we are born, we don't even have a past. It is all going to start now. There is a fresh beginning. We are not aware of how earthly life is going to be, how technologically advanced the earth has become, what good or bad the world holds and how dangerous the planet has become. We don't even have an identity yet; everyone calls us by sweet pet names, which sound good to them. We are not even aware that we are going to die someday, leaving everything behind.

We are busy crying. Every other living entity is a stranger to us.We can't even walk and talk. (Because we won't have an Idea SIM card when we are born!) We have a blank and peaceful mind. There are no worries and no responsibilities.We are expected to do only three things: drink milk, cry and sleep. Sleep for sixteen to twenty hours a day. Everything will be taken care of without us even asking. We don't have any problems. We don't have girlfriend problems (just kidding!). We don't need money, fame or success. No one expects anything from us. We will be treated like a crown prince or princess.

People try to talk to us and communicate with us using words and actions that make no sense to us at all. We wonder what he or she is actually trying to tell us. We become the centre of attraction. Everyone wants to carry us and play with us. We gradually start comprehending what they are trying to tell us. We don't understand anything in the beginning. Later on, we slowly start to learn by imitation.

Every new thing or person we see appears new, strange, interesting, beautiful, a bit scary, amazing and confusing. We have only two emotions: happiness and uneasiness. If someone makes us happy, we feel good and we smile. If we have had a sound sleep, then we are playful. If we are hungry, haven't had a good sleep, feel uneasiness in our stomach or we don't like the person carrying us, we cry. We cry if someone or something is making us feel uncomfortable. We don't care who or what it is. We are brave enough to reject what we don't like.

We feel lonely in the initial days. We don't know who our parents are or who our brother or sister is? We don't know who our family is or relatives are. We don't have any friends yet, other than a few toys. We are never left alone on our own. We wonder what is happening around us. Slowly as the days pass by, we start getting adjusted to the environment. Soon we realize that there is one person who is always with us, feeds us, makes us feel good, takes care of us, sings to us, talks to us, plays with us, takes us to the water, never does anything that we don't like and makes sure we have enough sleep and are not disturbed by anything or anyone while we are sleeping. We feel very much comfortable when she is around and no other person loves us the way she does. For us, she is the whole world. And we are her only world. We don't know yet that she is our mother and she gave birth to us.

We gradually start crawling and talking gibberish. We imitate what others tell us. As days pass by, we learn how to sit, stand and walk by holding the tables and walls. One day, we find ourselves running all over the place. By this time, we are pretty much aware of the things around us, whom to ask what we want, where to go and what to do. So many pretty girls kiss us, without us asking for them. They too ask us to kiss them. We get the feeling that the world revolves around us and we are the source of all happiness. The kissing rate will gradually come down as we grow. There comes a day when it will stop. And we don't understand why. We will be considered way too old to be kissed by the random beautiful girls. Have you ever wondered where all these beautiful girls went when we grew up?

If we are the first child, then we get a lot attention. We are the centre of attraction till the second child is born. Once we have a younger brother or sister, the older ones tend to get a bit jealous of their siblings, as they don't get the same attention as before. Now there is someone else to be taken care of. But as things settle down, we get a little older and a little wiser, we start playing with our little siblings, we feel good to be with them as now we have a companion all the time.

In our early childhood days, we are not afraid of anyone or anything. If we desire something, we just want it. We scream, shout, cry and do what it takes to make that thing ours. We don't give up or compromise. Similarly, if we don't want something we are forced with, we are daring enough to reject it. If someone we don't like carries us, we react immediately to get away from that person. If we don't appreciate what they are feeding us, then we won't eat it; we are heroic enough to spit it out (even on their face!) We don't give a damn about where we are, who are around us and what they will think about us. We are the kings of our own world.

Gradually, we are restricted from doing certain things. People impose rules upon us such as don't go there, don't do that, don't touch that, don't speak like that, don't eat that, don't play with that, you can't have everything you want and so on. We slowly stop doing the things we once did. However, we do certain things despite being forbidden to do so. We like doing it, so we do it, thinking we are born just to do this thing. These activities include chewing the thumb, eating mud, throwing things around, biting people when we get teeth, playing in water and playing weird games that our elders will never understand.

The best thing is this: we enjoy each and every passing moment and we are happy all the time. We sleep when we want to and eat whatever excites our taste buds. We don't want to eat what we are fed; we prefer eating toys, leaves, mud, dirt, coins, paper, plastic and clothes. Almost everything seems to be a beautiful thing to eat. Who cares whether it's healthy or dangerous? We just like the way it tastes. Yum!

As we grow older, a new character is introduced to us. People don't give a complete picture about him, but they seem to be very strict about this character. We don't have much of a choice other than to listen and believe in what they are saying. All that we know is this: His name is God; He lives in heaven. Neither do we see Him nor does He show up in front of us. We just need to believe in what they are saying, we have to. They will show us a reference image of how He looks like.

All we are expected to do is pray, ask Him for what we want, worship him, believe and trust that He exists and He will give us all that we ask for. No more questions. We are told that once we die, if we have done good things, He will take us to heaven and we can stay happily forever, eating bread and honey with him. If we do bad things, He will send us to hell, we are threatened. We are told hell is a horrible place and there is suffering. We are told that we will be punished for all the bad things we have done on earth. Uncle Yamaraj is a man with no sympathy; he may even fry us depending on the intensity of our crimes and sins. Elders literally scare us right from our childhood. If we don't eat, they say ghosts would take us away. Till date no one has come. They just made a fool of us to make sure we eat and do good things out of fear.

Everything goes on fine. We are still happy; we still don't have any tensions, responsibilities and work to do. We just eat, sleep, play, sing, dance, do a little circus, scream, bite, get irritated, fight, cry and run around. We are jobless until that disastrous day in our life when we join school.

We wonder *why this is happening to me?*

What is this place? Who is she and what is she trying to tell me? What is all this nonsense ABCD and 123? I was happier not knowing any of this for all my life. Why do you force me to learn new things and ruin my happiness?

We have to go to school every day. No matter how much we protest, cry, throw tantrums and perform a drama, our parents don't listen to us. They don't seem to give up. They are very strict about us going to school.

We are now expected to do things we never did before. We are expected to do things on our own. Our parents won't even wash our ass anymore. Soon enough, we lose our freedom to pee on the bed; all of a sudden it is considered a crime. We are now expected to go to the washroom even if it is the middle of the night and it is dark and scary around and we are very sleepy.

We have to get up early in the morning and go to school. We have to learn, make new friends, come home and do our homework. We can't play all the time anymore. Things start getting pretty serious. After a while, we get comfortable with this new life. We are constantly told that we are not little kids anymore.

Without our notice, our body grows big, we have learnt so much and we are aware of so many things. We have to study, whether we like it or not. We don't have a choice.

What a cosy life we led a few years ago! Look how life has turned out for us! How we were and what we have become! Now there are so many responsibilities and things to do. We try to be independent. Day by day, the burden of studies increases. The mathematics textbook is full of problems. Once upon a time, drawing was for fun; now we are forced to draw amoeba, graphs, heart, cells, digestive system, geometric diagrams and so on. Many new subjects are added along the way. Soon we fall into the trap of competition with our classmates. We want to be better than others in every aspect. This journey adds new emotions to us such as anger, jealousy, cursing and rivalry.

We slowly begin to experience new things in our body. We get a bit scared in the beginning because of all the weird things happening to us in weird places. We ask our friends whether it is all normal and is happening to them too. We wonder if we are the only victims of strange phenomena that are happening all of a sudden, out of nowhere. Soon we realise that we have matured. We have grown up and we are in our teenage.

During this phase in our life, a magical and fascinating thing happens. It increases our heartbeat but reduces the rpm of the brain. This feeling is popularly known and widely accepted as 'love.' First love is always special, it is unforgettable. Even if love doesn't happen, we at least have a few crushes. We are not sure what is happening with our hormones, but it is a good feeling of racing hearts and butterflies in our stomach. Experiences teach us new things; we have to think, make decisions, judge the good from the bad. We learn new things from our friends, hang out with them, bunk classes, go out and start exploring the world with them.

Soon enough, we get into college. We forget our first love and start looking for the second, third and fourth love. Our heart is filled with so much of love that one person doesn't seem to be enough for us to share our infinite love with. We want to give more and more love. This is also the time when we have to choose what we want to do for the rest of our life. The subjects we choose decide the path of our life. If we put in efforts and work hard at this point, the rest of our life will be good. Some become lazy and regret it for their lifetime. It is purely a matter of choice.

We have not only grown up, but our tensions, problems and responsibilities too have grown up with us. We have so much to be worried about and there is so much to take care of: our future life, career, higher studies, money, fame, success, happiness, love, relationships and break-ups.

What is right and what is wrong? Which university to choose for our master's? Which is the right career for us? Who is the right partner? How do we settle down in life? What would possibly keep us happy, which is the right track?

In the process, we will make a lot of mistakes, get into trouble at times, make some bad choices, indulge in bad habits, become a party animal, lose control over life, show no seriousness towards life, lose focus or get disoriented from our career and goals. One fine day, we will start learning from our mistakes. Gradually.

When we were children, we always wanted to grow up. Now that we have grown up, we realize that growing up was a trap, nothing else. We want to be a kid again. After graduation, the quest for a job follows. Do we take up the job that provides a steady cash flow and security or follow our dream to start a business?

By the time we make our decision and get used to life, we are old enough to face a big, risky, dangerous and outrageously obvious thing called… Yes, you guessed it right - 'Marriage!' And then parenthood. No one is ever ready to be a parent, but before we know it, we are the father or mother of two kids. Everything seems to happen way too fast. Everything passes by like a flash.

Now, there are better things to worry about: spouse and kids. We have to earn more money, be responsible, serious and stand by our family in the good and bad times. We also have to take care of our parents in their old age. No more night-outs and hanging out with friends like we used to. Weekends are meant to clean the house, take our children to the park and movies and do grocery shopping. The flirty romantic lover boy turns into a silent husband and a gentle father.

If you want to change the world, then change it before getting married. Because after marriage, you won't even get the chance to change the channel on television. Almost everyone I know says that marriage is tough and we lose all our freedom. But I guess it all depends on whom we choose as our spouse. Make a wise decision; we have to live with the person for the rest of our life. Yeah, we can divorce them, but instead of having so many complications in life, it is better to make a good decision right at the beginning.

There is a lot of debate over whether one should opt for love or an arranged marriage. Each has its own advantages and disadvantages. In love marriage, we marry our girlfriend. In an arranged marriage, we marry someone else's girlfriend. We just need to understand that nobody is perfect. We have to deal with each other's imperfections, respect and understand them. They say everything will be fine once we have kids. I don't know about that. I don't have an experience in marriage.

One day we will be old. That will happen sooner than we thought. And we begin to wonder how everything passed by so quickly. All we have now are the memories of life so far. We can't go back and fix a thing. We may have some regrets that we should have done this instead of that, we should have married the person we loved or we should have lived our dreams and so on. But we chose this life. We may also wish that we had forgiven everyone. In the end, nothing is going to matter. We may also wish we shouldn't have bothered about what people thought about us and had done what we wanted to do. We may wonder why we were so afraid of what other people thought of us. The clock is ticking and we can only wonder, but we cannot do anything about the past now.

Our children too will go through the same phases that we and our father had been through. They too learn everything from scratch: crawl, walk, run, talk, go to school, get a degree, job, marry, have kids and so on… As they say: Life is a… "EXACTLY!" And then we die someday. As simple as that. No reasons, excuses, fake promises, hidden charges, terms and conditions. No sorry and no thank you. Your story may be different, but the climax is one and the same: "**DEATH!**"

Try to be alive; you have to die someday.

Yeah… Eventually we all do!

THE DEAD-END!

Regardless of how good or bad it is, life will always come to an end. So will this book. Nothing is ever built to last. Thank you for reading this book. I hope it made at least a tiny impact on you in some way or the other. I am very sorry if you found this book rude or offensive in any way. But I am sure at least some of you had a good time reading it. So how was the journey? Was it worthwhile? Do you want to read it again? LOL, just asking!

Well, I have successfully completed this book by the age of twenty-four. I guess I wouldn't have been so happy and fulfilled if I had written a senti-mental happy ending love story, a novel or non-fiction. It took around ten months to write this book. I am officially a writer now. I didn't know how to write, but this book taught me how to write. Writing is really a lot of fun. With this experience, I will be a better writer in future. I already have five to six titles ready in my head. Don't worry, they aren't about life, especially not about death. It is really amazing how the brain works. You just have to believe and start doing it. Initially it sucks, but it just keeps getting better and better as it unleashes its power, slowly making you invincible. All you have to do is keep doing it and never give up.

No one knows what is exactly right and wrong or what is true and what is false. It is entirely up to you to decide. This book is the combined effort of all those thoughts, reading, imagination, hours of conversations, debates, arguments and experiences as I dug deep into the mystery of life and death. This book is a result of my life experiences till today, others' stories, guidance and support.

This book has given me the confidence to write more books. It has made me a better person and has given a sense of achievement. I will make sure my next book isn't offensive to anybody in anyway. All the chapters in this book may not have sounded good to everybody; even our Sachin Tendulkar doesn't score a century in every cricket match. I tried my best not to make you feel bored, but I do not know how interesting the book was to you. Did you fall asleep anywhere?

Thank you for your valuable time, money and patience to read this book and still reading it… Was it worth your time and money? If yes, then I hope you look forward to my next book. I may need another year to release it.

I hope you had a wonderful time reading this book. If you liked this book, then please recommend it to your family, friends, colleagues, co-workers, neighbours and, if possible, to your enemies too. Let everyone discover the combined weight of life and death. If you did not like the book for any reason, tell me why. I look forward to your feedback, both positive and negative. Do let me know how your overall experience reading this book was. Write your review online. I will use your feedback as the foundation for my upcoming books. I sign off here.

Thanks a million!

For questions, debates, arguments, compliments, complaints, suggestions and rants,

Write to: gavindsouza.theauthor@gmail.com

- Gavin D'Souza

The Writer's Note

Well, I wrote a whole book about it. I researched, asked questions and found some of the answers (these maybe just a few drops in the mighty ocean). Death still amazes me. I still have questions. I have no clue whom to ask. Why should I even ask? Is what I have written in harmony with what actually happens or is it totally out of the league? Like, once we are dead, we're dead and that's it? One can only presume. We won't be alive to see if it is all true.

With advancement in technology, will we be able to someday cheat death and live forever? Even if the answer is yes, will we be alive to see it happen? Is there any point in raising all these questions? Did these questions mean something to you? Did you understand what I was trying to convey? Do you have any questions?

I have edited this book over and over many times. I have read every word several times. I have deleted, replaced, changed, added, improvised and modified many words. How far have I been successful in conveying my thoughts? I don't know. Did reading this book make you wonder about something? Are you confused? Too many questions, right? Why aren't you closing the book yet? Are you expecting something? Maybe a "senti-mental happy ending?" Do you want a few tears gushing down your cheeks to gush down all those heavy emotions…? Will that make you feel lighter, warmer and comfortable? Well…

Stage 33

What if You Don't Wake Up *Alive Tomorrow Morning?*

There is something about death that is comforting.
The thought you could die tomorrow frees you to appreciate your life now.

- Angelina Jolie

It is just another ordinary night, like any of the other nights. You are in deep sleep, comfortably tucked into your soft spongy mattress, your head resting on a mellow pillow, your body covered with a thick blanket. The clock strikes three in the middle of the night. The fast spinning fan that kept you cool all this while stops rotating. The blades don't slow down as it always does, they come to complete halt in an instant. The lights turn on. Everything becomes calm; there is profound pindrop silence. You feel that your blanket is slowly being pulled away by an external unknown force.

The night sets into motion with you getting ready with a thick fur coat and a big backpack. You start your heroic journey with sheer dynamic passion. In that blazing chilly snowfall night, you climb up a cliff for a long time, enduring a lot of breathing difficulties, tiredness, continuous panting, furious heart beats three times a second and a dry throat. There is barely any stamina left in you. You peep into your backpack for a *Red Bull* energy drink, as you desperately need some 'wings' to reach your destination. You won't find one, yet you are not giving up. There is only one place at the top. You want to reach there by hook or crook, alive in one piece. After a long time of trekking through the clouds, the dawn paves its way, clearing the fog for a breath-taking view of the highest point on the planet – Mount Everest, the heaven on earth.

You have almost made it to the top. You are just a few steps away from reaching your final destination. With your momentum running out, you try to climb faster and higher. You have almost reached the top. Suddenly, you are attacked by the strong side winds, blowing at a speed of 69 km an hour, forcing you backwards, away from the mountain. Unable to cope up with the rustling wind, you start losing control at the height of 29,000 feet above the sea level. The heavy backpack behind you is making things worse. Your left leg slips on a small stone. You lose balance and slowly start your decent. You roll all the way downhill. You push past the heavy winds and snow, trying to hold on to something. You desperately try to stop the rapid decent. On the way down, you somehow manage to open your eyes wide open, only to find yourself in your bedroom.

You get up, sweating as though you are on Kalahari Desert in the blazing heat of the sun on a hot summer afternoon. Then you get back your senses to see an old man, 7.3 feet tall, with long golden hair and a thick white beard, wearing a pure glowing white suit, staring at you. You are amazingly stunned, shockingly surprised and astonishingly horrified to see this strange man eating an apple. The windows and doors of the room are safely locked from the inside. You still haven't returned from the Himalayas. And this man is in your room, out of nowhere, in the middle of the night.

You are not only scared, but afraid too. You slowly open your mouth to break the silence. You stutter. Gathering some words, you speak with a shaky voice.

"Who the hell are you man? Why are you sitting and eating an apple in my room in the middle of the night? Wh...What do you want? Don't harm me, take all you want."

The old beardy man finishes his apple from the orchids of Cupertino, California, gets up from the chair and starts roaming around the room. He looks into your eyes. Then he speaks with a bold, serious, thick and magnificent voice.

"Yes son, I am here to take away everything that you have."

He stares at you with his powerful eyes that never blink. They are always open and staring at you. You ask him nervously.

"Well, what do you even want from me?"

Instead of an answer, you get a question from him.

"What do you have, son? What can you give me?"

You start pointing at the things in your room.

"There is uhhh...a TV, a computer, clothes in the closet, money and jewellery in the locker. (Pause) Back home, there is a refrigerator, washing machine, utensils and all the other household items. (Long pause) My car is parked outside. The keys are in the drawer. You want my mobile too?"

"Son, are all these things yours? Did you bring them when you came to the earth?"

You turn your head to the left and see that the door is still locked. You wonder if there any way to escape,

"Anh? No, no, I bought them here on earth, man. On EMI with my credit card (making a frown face) and still paying the bills. How can I bring them while coming to the earth? Are there any shopping malls out there?"

After thinking for a while, you continue.

"Sir, are you from the… uhhh…income tax department by any chance? Well, I really don't possess anything illegal or any black money, I swear. There are bigger thieves and politicians you should be really concentrating on. I am not the right guy for this. No!"

"Well, I am not from the income tax department. What is this income tax department? I don't need all these material earthly things of yours, son. They are absolutely of no use to me," he says.

Now you begin to get confused.

"Then what is it that you want? Who are you, why are you here? To scare the shit out of me? This isn't funny, man!"

With a little smile on his face, he says, "I am the one, creator of heaven and earth, alpha and omega. I am God! I created you, son. I gave you thy life."

With a breaking voice, you say, "Wow! You are God? Seriously? All my life I thought you were invisible. Whoa! You are a huge man. What's your… How tall are you? Seven feet? Unbelievable! Uhhh… By any chance is this another dream just like the Everest one? Because, trust me when I say this, I have already had enough for the night."

"Yes, I am the one. I am invisible, son, but I am not blind. No, this isn't any sort of a dream. This is happening for real. I am here for you, son."

"How cute! That's so sweet of you God. You came all the way down from heaven just to see me? (Pause) I can't believe it. That's interesting. I never thought I would see you in my lifetime. Or else I would have been prepared with a long wish list of things I want from you. It's okay, just give me some time… I will come up with something. Sure, I need a number of things. Just wondering where to start… (Long pause) Wow God! This is awesome, man! I never thought you would come personally to fulfil my wishes. So you had some free time and you thought of visiting me? Hmm…When was the last time I prayed so much that you became so much impressed with me?"

"That's the problem son, you never believe."

He continues, "I am not here to fulfil your wishes. I am here not to give you anything. As I said, I am here to take everything of yours."

"Now, wait a minute… (trying to be smart ass in front of God), you said you don't need any of the…"

You raise both your hands and do the double quote with your fingers. "Earthly things…"

"And now you want everything of mine? What are you trying to tell me Mr. God, or whatever? This is completely insane! What will you do with my fridge, TV and washing machine, man? I am not going to give my mobile at any cost."

With a broad smile, he says, "I am here for your life, son! That is what I meant by…" He too raises both his hands (imitating you) to do the double quote. "Everything."

"You must be kidding, right? I mean… Are you really God? You mean that *God*, God? Why me? *Why is it always the good guys?* You can't be serious. Why today? Why so early? You can't just show up out of nowhere and end my life, just like that! Can you? (Pausing and thinking) I still haven't done anything valuable yet, God. I have big dreams. Are you doing this to me just because I wasn't praying enough? Is that the reason behind all this? I mean, really? Ok… Okay, from tomorrow, I will pray for… (Thinking) three hours. I skip one or two meals for you… I'll… I'll… I'll take care of my family well. I won't do any harm or bad to others. I'll change. Give me a chance, just one chance. I will never commit a sin again. Please don't take my life. I want to live. Please! I have a family to take care of. I have people relying on me, I have…"

"I am afraid it is already too late to apologise, son. All these days you had the opportunity, but what were you doing? It has to happen someday, son. It is happening today. I am not here because you were not praying and fulfilling my expectations. You don't have to sacrifice, give or do anything. It makes no difference. I am God for heaven's sake. I have the power to do anything, in fact everything that I want to do. Instead of praying and fasting, do something good for the poor and the needy people. Help thy brothers, sisters, family and friends. Forgive your enemies. That is why I put you here on earth. To serve! You aren't utilising your life properly, son. You are just wasting it."

You open your mouth and just stare at God with your eyes popping out.

God continues, "I haven't sent you here to lie, get angry, stop talking to people, disrespect elders, get jealous of others' growth, take revenge, fight, think about yourself and make money. I gave a chance to you all these days, but you never changed and I don't think you ever will. All of humanity is just getting out of control. Frankly, I am sick and tired of all this. I have decided to end it, end it my way. Which is why I give you no control over death. If I have the right to give you life, then I have the right to take it back, whenever I want to."

"Don't do this, dude. Yes, I made some bad choices and mistakes. I was busy when my friends needed me, but who isn't? You cannot keep taking everyone's life for that. Then there will be no single human on planet earth. Will there be? Be honest. Well, I know you can't… you won't lie."

You think God may need some time to answer this question. But God speaks up instantly as soon as you close your lip.

"Yes son, everyone makes mistakes. I agree with you. Yesterday was somebody's turn; tomorrow will be somebody else's. But tonight it is yours, son. All yours! Every human being has a day. Everyone gets a chance to live, learn from their past mistakes, lead a better life than yesterday and finally come back to me one day."

You have no clue what to think or say. You are silently staring at God, with a tear rolling on your left cheek.

"Son, you seem to be good at heart. Are you?"

"Yes, yes, I am! Give me a chance, God. I'll make it up to you this time. Uhhhhh… Everyone deserves a second chance. In fact, I am… Nothing, nothing… Let us negotia…"

"Fine, fine. Enough of your Shakespeare dramas. I get that from everyone. But you have to convince me. You must give me three clear, convincing and valid reasons why I should let you live tonight and not take thy life right away, RIGHT NOW!!!"

"What are your three reasons?"

—THAT'S ALL FOLKS!—